you are
WORTHY!

Even When You Believe Otherwise

A GUIDE FOR THE
OVERWHELMED PERFECTIONIST

Gloria,
What a treat to have
you in my life! Keep
shining your light! You
are helping our world
thrive! Love,
Julee

JULEE HUNT

Praise for *You are WORTHY!*

Julee walks her talk every day and through this she has created a straightforward and gentle way to determine if your worthiness is off-line and the triggers that lead to or repeat any lack of worthiness. Her book is a "how to" guide to discover your worthiness. Her experience is real and her insights are compassionate as they lead you to healing and activating your worthiness to attract your best life. Julee has helped me beyond measure through her sincere and raw experience, knowledge, and practices. The empowering new habits she suggests are doable and rewarding in the moment. While it may feel overwhelming to recover from unworthiness, this book makes it possible. I am worthy and so are you!

~ **Anni Kemp, Intentional Artist and founder of Intentional Graffiti™**

This book is filled with practical tools you can use immediately to activate the best version of you and live your best life. Julee gives you brilliant tools to transform your "FUD" into personal power to create a life you love."

~ **Andy Dooley, creator of Vibration Activation™**

I have known Julee for over 20 years and have watched her create an amazing, unique, and fulfilling life. This book is the experience of her evolution. What I love most are the powerful, thought provoking, productive, and life transforming tools as well as the many resources that she includes. You can't help feeling worthy if you implement just some of the tools presented in this book.

~ Rev. Carole O'Connell, Author of *The Power of Choice: 10 Steps to a Joyous Life*

In this groundbreaking new book, the concept of worthiness is fully explored. It offers a deep insight into the feelings of being unworthy and the high cost on the individual, the family, and society itself. The good news is that just as unworthiness has been learned, it can be "unlearned". This book gives you the tools to finally free yourself from feeling unworthy. There is a brighter life waiting for you and this book can help you get there.

~ Michael Tarby, Author of *Living Your Big Juicy Life; The Secrets to Having More Love, Joy and Success*

If you are feeling some unpleasant emotions, stuck in habits or behaviors that aren't serving you, or just feeling depleted, you may be affected by the cycle of unworthiness! This book captures the serious consequences of growing up looking outside of ourselves for validation and how to believe in our intrinsic worth. Julee's inspiring and courageous journey is filled with relatable anecdotes, gems of wisdom, and real easy to follow tools that you can use to make a significant change in how you feel about your life.

~ **Regena Garrepy, Speaker, Leadership Coach, Retreat Facilitator**

FOREWORD

The book you are holding in your hand will take you on the greatest adventure of your life. Knowing that you are worthy just because you exist trumps all other life lessons. The book that Julee has written walks you through a step by step process for deepening your self-worth.

I have known Julee for over twenty years, first as a parishioner at my church and then as my makeup consultant and friend. She is one of the most adventuresome people I know. I have been witness to her spiritual journey and the evolving of her confidence, self-esteem, and yes worthiness. When she told me that she and her family were going on an RV adventure with no idea where they would land, I was both thrilled and a little scared for them. What courage it took to step out of the conventional lifestyle box and jump with both feet into the adventure of a lifetime. It was a wise choice for them and one I know they will ever be grateful for following that creative idea.

Julee does a brilliant portrayal of how so many of us develop a sense of unworthiness and exactly how low self-worth looks and feels. In my many years of counselling, I have discovered that the familiar issues that we face whether we label them health, relationships, finances, career, the underlying cause is low self-worth. Our unworthiness which we learned from well-meaning people and cultures hinders everything we do in life. As

Julee explains, our worthiness drives all aspects of our life and when we don't feel good about ourselves, life takes on a feeling of disconnection.

I so appreciate Julee's vulnerability in sharing her personal experience of feeling unworthy and how that led to perfectionism and to workaholic behavior. Many of us can relate to her story. For those of us who grew up hearing that we were not good enough from our families, our culture, even our church, we applaud the theme of this book. She explains how and why we feel unworthy. Her story and examples resonate with us. We are there now or have possibly been down that road of low self-worth at some time in our life.

The second part of the book, which is my favorite, shares ideas, tools and techniques of how we can lift ourselves into a consciousness of high self-worth which is truly our birthright. The tool bag she creates for the reader is fabulous and complete. If you ever wanted to know what you could do to feel better about yourself, this book is for you.

I feel that I now have a resource for many of my clients who are struggling to climb that ladder out of unworthiness into a deep and profound belief in their own worthiness. Even though I have worked on my own level of self-worth, I found in some of the tools Julee shares a new and exciting way to see myself and my life from a higher perspective. Believing in our worthiness is a process that opens our heart, our vulnerability, our willingness to be real with ourselves and causes us to take responsibility for where we are now as adults. No matter what happened to us as children, we are at choice every moment of every day as adults to see ourselves and all of life differently. The really good news is that we have the ability, the power and the opportunity to make that shift into worthiness and experience the high joy that life is meant to be.

Rev. Carole O'Connell
Author of:
The Power of Choice
Seven Secrets to Abundant Living
The Adventures of CJ and Angel
www.caroleoconnell.com

DEDICATION

I dedicate this book to my loving husband, Dan, and my son, Austin. Their support, encouragement and belief in me make me a better person every day.

Thank you!

"Believe in Yourself | Love What You Do | Live Life Fully"

Julee Hunt

CONTENTS

ACKNOWLEDGEMENTS

Thank you, Dan, my loving husband and best friend, for believing in me and supporting me. I am grateful that you are my husband and life partner.

Thank you, Austin, my amazing son, for being an example of true leadership and encouragement to me and others. I am grateful for your unconditional love and support.

Thank you, Christy Hovey, for being one of my writing accountability partners early in the hatching of this idea. I am grateful for your friendship, encouragement, and your patience.

Thank you, Regena Garrepy, coach extraordinaire, for encouraging me to share my story in order to help others heal. I am grateful for your loving heart, encouragement, and wise wisdom. You help me see things differently!

Thank you to my Red Hot Visionista Soul Sisters who gave me a safe place to heal the wounds of my childhood. I am grateful for your unconditional love and acceptance even when I could not do that for myself.

Thank you to Cy Gilbert, photographer extraordinaire who easily captures the essence of each person he photographs. My cover turned out great because of your stellar photo!

Thank you to my writing coach and editor, Madeleine Eno, who helped me take this book from idea to reality and kept me accountable to my goals. Your editing and encouragement helped me see this through to fruition.

INTRODUCTION

We're experiencing an epidemic in our world today that has silently slipped into the mainstream world while we were unconscious. It's leading us down a path toward catastrophic events that could take decades or even generations to recover from.

This epidemic has caused:

- Our society to stop dreaming and lose faith in possibilities.
- People to play small, live rote lives, and feel hopeless.
- Pervasive blame and lack of responsibility.
- Depression on such a level that we have thousands of drugs to combat it.
- Addictions to alcohol, drugs, food, porn, shopping, social media, TV… the list goes on forever.
- Negativity and focus on what is wrong with the world rather than what is right.
- Unkindness toward others and ourselves.
- Loss of diversity and tolerance, resulting in never-ending wars and hate crimes.

The epidemic?

Unworthiness.

In my work as a coach I listen to people's stories. And I hear from far too many people who are struggling because they are unable or unwilling to acknowledge their own worthiness and the importance it plays in the outcome of their life. They are more willing to compare themselves to someone else and look at *others* as worthy before they will admit they, too, are worthy. They are busy looking for worthiness outside themselves instead of within, where it truly lives.

You are born worthy. In fact, you were born in the image and likeness of God, with the highest level of worthiness there is. The mere fact that a sperm and egg came together and created YOU, a miracle of life, makes you worthy to take up space on the planet.

Along the way, you learned unworthiness—and if it was learned it can be *unlearned.*

So how has feeling unworthy become the norm? Well, pressures from society, parents, religion, and educational institutions play a big part. We've all had well-meaning people in our lives who installed thoughts and beliefs throughout our childhood. While some of these beliefs empower us most of them remind us that we're not enough—that we're unworthy of success, happiness, health, and the dreams our hearts desire.

Are you thinking you had good parents who raised you well? That may be, but for a moment, think back to how you were rewarded as a child.

Did your parents:

- Ask you to clean your room and when you did, praise you for doing what they asked?
- Praise you when you brought home a report card with all As?
- Reward you with ice cream when you scored the winning goal?

So far so good….

But did they also:

- Punish you for not doing what they asked?
- Tear you down or show their disappointment when you got a B on your report card?
- Withhold ice cream when you did not win the game or get first place in a race or competition?

That is what I call "conditional worthiness." Only when you do well, are you worthy. The message is: "I will love and accept you when you do exactly what I ask." If you do anything less than perfect or make a mistake, parents often withhold their love, even very subtly, which will make any kid question their worth. The training for seeking approval, love, and worthiness outside yourself begins right here.

You're born perfect! Then you're fed a whole array of messages that make you believe you are less than perfect or unworthy—and you spend most of your life trying to do just about *anything* to become perfect again. That's where you get into trouble.

For instance, the media installs beliefs into you that make you think you are less-than, unless:

- You've got six-pack abs.
- You have a gorgeous mate and tons of friends.
- You are wrinkle-free, gray-free, and fat-free.

Advertisers want you to believe that you are not worthy unless you use their product. A product that will, by the way, make your life perfect (just the way it was when you were born).

This makes you start to play the "When I…" game. It goes like this: "I'll be worthy when I…"

- lose ten pounds.
- get the college degree.
- promote to the next level.
- make lots of money.
- get married.
- have children.

But what if none of these things ever happen? You never lose the ten pounds, make lots of money, or have children? Does that make you unworthy?

NO, IT DOES NOT! You are worthy even without all those things. And the problem is, even if you do get them, the worthiness bar keeps moving.

Let's say your "When I…" is making it to the top rung of the corporate ladder. You spend years absolutely *certain* that as you make it to each rung you become more worthy. All is going well until the day you get laid off.

How do you react?

If your worthiness was tied to that job and your climb up the ladder, when the job (and the ladder) goes away, your worthiness goes with it—at least in your mind.

I know this one from personal experience and can tell you that your worth is not gone, no matter what happens. It always lies within you and is waiting for you to honor and acknowledge it. When you do, you see that the things outside you have nothing to do with your worthiness. Worthiness is like an old friend just waiting for you to come and visit. It will never let you down as long as you feed it internally!

That's what this book is all about.

Our world is farther off track than we are willing to admit and it's a result of this unworthiness epidemic. The thing is, it's hard to see it when we're in the middle of it. You've heard that saying, "The fish doesn't know it's wet."

One thing we don't quite see is that we have more information at our fingertips than ever before. You may be wondering how search engines, social media, TV, movies, radio, blogs, and books can make you feel unworthy. Well, the constant bombardment does not give you any time to process what you've received before new information arrives. Not only is this overwhelming, but it also gives you more opportunity to compare yourself with everyone else and wonder if you measure up.

When I first started my corporate career, the internet didn't exist. When I needed to research I went to the library. It was a slow and tedious process, but it gave my mind time to process the information and get clear on my search. Today our minds don't have time to process anything—and they are so distracted. Rather than systematically looking through the information to find what you need and form an opinion, your scattered mind tries to determine where you fit into the information you received and wonder, "Am I enough?"

Our world is on a detour that if not corrected will only lead to more conflicts and violence. Our current President feels it is OK to speak words of unkindness into any person, group, or belief system that docs not agree with him. Look, the fact that the most disrespectful candidate can become president while white supremacist groups hold public rallies protesting African Americans and Muslims tells us we've got a long way to go toward recognizing the worthiness of each and every human being.

The increasing incidence of bullying and violence in schools, online, and even on our roadways; the negativity in the finger-pointing news and social media; and the way you talk to yourself are all more evidence of a growing unworthiness epidemic.

When you feel unworthy, you attack others. You blame someone else for your crummy life. You become complacent about social injustice and watch while people are so poorly treated. You look outside yourself for your worthiness and become part of a cycle that has caused prejudice, political unrest, and wars that never end.

There is much healing still to be done. And the way to heal our world is to start with your own worthiness.

The bottom line: If you do not see your own worthiness, it's difficult for you to see it in others. In fact, if you do not feel worthy, it would be a double standard for you to ask others to see in you something you don't see in yourself.

You have a choice. By seeing and honoring your own worthiness you help create a society that functions from a place of worthiness. This means you see your own worth and can see it in other people.

This book is for you if you:

- Feel hopeless instead of hopeful.
- Are depressed and can't see a way out.
- Play the "When I…" game.
- Are addicted to drugs, alcohol, food, social media, TV, porn —anything in excess.
- Consistently compare yourself to others and never quite measure up.
- Look at yourself and the world through a lens of "impossible" instead of "possible."
- Never get your hopes up.
- Have a high FUD factor: Fear, Uncertainty, and Doubt.
- Are unwilling or unable to make decisions.

I want you to have hope and be encouraged. You learned unworthiness and can unlearn it. You get to be the student as you begin to honor the worthiness that resides inside you. Your worthiness has been waiting a long time for you to acknowledge it and it's ready to ignite at any moment— when you are ready.

I know this one well because I, too, learned to look for my worthiness outside myself. I believed if I got the college degree and worked my ass off at a good job, *then* I would be worthy of taking up space on our planet. I wanted others to see my worth so I worked sixty to eighty hours a week, traveled fifty percent of my time for the company, and gave up my personal life for a soul-sucking job. I thought I was more worthy because of how much harder I worked than everyone else. That is, up until the day I was invited to leave my job. That's right—I was laid off.

The next morning, I woke up devastated, lost, embarrassed, and feeling *worthless*. In fact, my entire identity and worthiness were still sitting at the desk I had left the day before. From the outside, it looked like I had the perfect life. But in reality, my marriage was on the rocks, my health was failing, and I had zero social life.

After nursing my wounds, I set out on a journey to discover my worthiness. In this book, I'll share everything I learned along the way.

By reading this book you will learn to look at things differently and start to see the miracles that surround you every day. You'll learn the wisdom and healing power in your story for yourself and for others. You will see how the events of your life have prepared you for what's next: the detours, adversities, positive and negative days, losses and gains have been on purpose and not for naught. You will learn that feelings of hopelessness are an invitation to learn and grow. You will learn how powerful you are and how you can use that power to create a life you love.

By tapping into your own worthiness, you make the world a better place to be for yourself and others. When you recognize and honor your own worthiness, you have the power to change the events of our world and help it get back on track.

No one was put on this earth to live a life of quiet desperation. The worthiness stirring in your soul has been waiting for you to sit up and take notice. With worthiness comes more joy, love, and abundance. Igniting your worthiness empowers you to create a life you can't wait to jump out of bed and live every day—a life of purpose, meaning, joy, and lots of fun and laughter.

I'm so glad you're joining me on this journey and choosing NOT to be a statistic in the unworthiness epidemic.

UNWORTHINESS

Chapter One: What is Unworthiness?

When I was twenty-five I decided to get my private pilot license. I was fascinated with the idea, felt it was an ambitious goal, and thought it would be badass to be a pilot. I completed ground school and started my lessons in the air. After a few hours of air time, the instructor said it was time to learn how to "fly under the hood." This is when they pull a big visor down low on your brow so you can't see out the window in front of you. You're forced to fly by your instruments only. It simulates flying on a cloudy day when you can't see more than a few inches or feet in front of you and feels like driving in a thick fog. But it's way scarier being several thousand feet in the air.

To me, living with unworthiness feels very much like flying under the hood. You're in a fog, with no visibility. You're scared, anxious, and waiting for something bad to happen. Because you can't see more than a few inches in front of your face, you're blind to the opportunities right before you.

This is how unworthiness holds you back from reaching your dreams. Without a sense of worth, people lack self-love and self-confidence. They compare themselves to others and never measure up. The unworthy individual looks outside herself for approval, acceptance, and love, and rarely finds them. Decision-making is torture for the unworthy individual. She seeks the advice of others before pulling the trigger on any decision—and often never even decides.

The unworthy also fear being found out. You might be one of those people, like I used to be, who pretends you're fine to the outside world, but can't wait to get home, close the door, and let down your guard. You are like a duck, calm on top of the water, but underneath your feet are pedaling like mad to gain approval and love, and keep yourself afloat.

Operating this way is exhausting and inauthentic. Your day might go like this: Wake up to your alarm clock still tired, intravenously pour coffee into your body, put on all your masks, paste on a smile, and head into the world. At the end of the day you're spent from pretending to be something you are not. When you go to bed, you think about all the things you did not finish and did not say. You feel dejected, berate yourself, and close your eyes vowing that tomorrow you will try to do things differently. You wake up remembering your vow, but by 10 a.m. your FUD (Fear, Uncertainty, Doubt) has been stirred up and your whole day is out of control and ruined once again. You repeat the process day in and day out.

Does this cycle sound familiar?

Am I Unworthy?

There are different levels of unworthiness—from debilitating paralysis to moderately functional. Just like alcoholism, no matter what level it has reached, alcohol is still impacting the alcoholic's life. Unworthiness works the same way.

My entire childhood was a training ground in unworthiness. I carried the lessons I learned into my adulthood. I suffered from perfectionism that kept me from enjoying life. I had trouble making decisions. What if it was not the right one? This constant need to make perfect decisions kept me frozen in fear and unable to move forward. When it came time to plan a vacation, the task felt overwhelming. I always focused on how much there was to do to make it happen instead of looking at the possibilities for fun and adventure. When we arrived at our destination, I was worn out from the unnecessary energy I expended trying to make it perfect. All I wanted to do was sleep.

And then there were our parties.

I'd start the planning weeks in advance. I had to

create the perfect guest list, the perfect menu, the perfect theme and decorations, and, of course, the house had to be perfect. One time this meant a new floor in the kitchen. My husband hated it when we had people over because I'd put a new list of home repairs and remodel projects on his plate, with unreasonable deadlines.

Then I'd work myself into the ground making sure that everything was perfect. By the time the guests arrived I felt like a wet dishrag ready to be wrung out and couldn't wait to go to bed.

At the end of each party, I would vow to never do it that way again. But the cycle of perfectionism was so ingrained that the very next time I would start out with good intentions, and end up in a frenzy. I was so far from creating a perfect life. In fact, perfectionism was *ruining* my life.

Besides perfectionism, there are a multitude of symptoms, cycles, or behaviors associated with unworthiness. As you read through these, think about where these might show up in your own life:

- Lack of self-confidence and self-love
- Playing small or having a desire to be invisible
- Low energy

- Often disappointed in yourself
- Negative, hopeless, or depressed
- Easily overwhelmed
- Lack of vision and inability to see possibilities
- Rarely happy
- Playing the "When I…" game
- Inauthenticity and pretending to be something you are not
- Inflexibility
- Always waiting for the other shoe to drop
- Comparing yourself to others and you never measure up
- Living in fear
- Suffering from insomnia or have trouble falling asleep
- Experiencing resistance in all areas of your life
- Difficulty making decisions
- Attacking other people in order to feel better about yourself
- Negative self-talk from your Inner Bully

Take the Unworthiness Test

Still unsure? Ask yourself these questions to help you determine if you are suffering from unworthiness. Check the box for YES, NO, or SOMETIMES.

	YES	NO	SOMETIMES
Do you look at the events happening in our world and feel hopeless?			
Do you want to make a difference but think you are not enough to have an impact?			
Do you buy things to make yourself feel better or eat unhealthy foods with the belief that they will fill your "I am not enough void"? (Maybe you don't even consciously know this is why you are overbuying or overeating.)			
Are you uncomfortable when someone gives you a compliment? Do you say, "This old thing" or "I got it on sale" shunning the compliment?			
Does it make you uncomfortable to look into our own eyes in the mirror, and say, "I love you"?			
Do you feel like you are living a life of quiet desperation?			

	YES	NO	SOMETIMES
Do you wish your life had more meaning or purpose?			
Are you wondering where the real you went—the one who felt alive, joyful, and excited about life? (Not the one who needs intravenous coffee to kick-start each day)			
Do you spend too much time completing the never-ending to-do list instead of enjoying the many pleasures life has to offer?			
Are you going to a job to pay your bills instead of filling your soul?			
Do you often think that when you have enough money, or lose enough weight, or find the right spouse, then and only then, you will be happy?			
Do you feel like a fraud pretending to have it all, but when you get home you are happy to close the door and leave the outside world behind?			

	YES	NO	SOMETIMES
Is your health failing?			
Is your marriage on the rocks?			
Do you have trouble making decisions?			

If you answered, "YES or SOMETIMES" to three or more of these questions, you have been taught conditional worthiness and learned to look for your worthiness outside yourself. You believe you're only worthy when you are perfect.

Congratulations! You are in good company. Conditional worthiness is not only common, it's also reversible. It doesn't mean you're sentenced to a life of misery.

How Did I Become Unworthy?

You were born worthy; you were taught how to be unworthy. Your well-meaning parents installed messages that either empowered you or made you feel unworthy. Some of the unworthiness you carry can also be the result of misperceptions of messages you picked up as a child.

For example, my parents felt it was important I learn that "Life is Hard." At first, I didn't believe them because my life started out pretty easy. Well, okay, coming through the birth canal was a bit tough, but once I was out, all I had to do was cry and someone would pick me up, cuddle me, feed me, or change me.

As I got older, getting good grades, making new friends, and excelling at sports all came easily to me. My parents kept telling me that life was hard, though, and finally, I took notice of what they were talking about.

I started watching their lives more closely. Sure enough, I could see that their lives were hard. They worked constantly. When they came home they took care of the four of us, feeding us, helping us with homework, and making sure we went to bed. At night, they'd fall into bed exhausted. On weekends, they shuttled all of us to our different activities. All they did was go, go, go with little time for rest, relaxation, and fun. From my observation and their persistence in telling me that "life is hard," I perceived that as an adult, things were going to be challenging.

That misperception was stored in my subconscious

as a child and when I became an adult, the switch flipped and, in the blink of an eye, life went from being easy to being hard. I could have perceived that their adult lives were easy and stored that into my subconscious. (That would have made things a whole lot simpler.) Instead I concluded that "life must be hard as an adult."

Now, no life is easy all the time. Losing a loved one, getting fired, receiving a scary diagnosis—these are difficult. But I make life harder than it needs to be by worrying about things I cannot change. I definitely make it harder when I add perfectionism to the equation. This usually adds additional steps and rigidity making things *really* hard, exhausting, and in the end, unnecessarily complicated. When I relax into the ebb and flow of life, and opt to be flexible, miracles can occur. This is so much easier than being in a constant state of fear and always trying to control the outcome.

Today I have a reminder on my calendar that says, "How can I make this easier?" I consciously and regularly remind myself to let life happen organically because the "hard" way is so ingrained in me. Regular tending to my mind is a tool I use to stay out of the unworthiness cycle.

Your parents are not the only ones that loaded up

your subconscious with thoughts that led you down the path of unworthiness. Your teachers, scout leaders, coaches, friends, friends' parents, aunts, uncles, grandparents, and ministers—along with an unhealthy dose of advertising, movies, and TV—all had the ability to steer you there, too.

To me, advertising has got to be the worst influence of all of these. Its goal is to make you feel "less than" unless you purchase a certain product, tapping right into the "When I..." game. (i.e., I will be whole, perfect, and complete when I use this shampoo, floor wax, or mascara.) This philosophy has led our society to amass credit card debt to the tune of $3.9 trillion dollars in the US alone [1]. Only fifteen countries have a GDP greater than that. That means the rest of the countries in the world have a GDP lower than what's owed to MasterCard and VISA by Americans.

Why do we have so much credit card debt? For me, my over-spending was driven by trying to fill the void of worthiness. I filled up an entire 4,000-square-foot home, closets, and cupboards, with items I purchased to make me feel better about myself—to make me feel worthy. By the time I was laid off, I

---

[1] www.valuepenguin.com

had racked up nearly $70,000 of credit card debt and I *still* felt unworthy. In fact, this figure ignited my itty bitty shitty committee and sent me into a tailspin of self-loathing, criticism, negativity, shame, blame, and guilt.

When I was a young adult I watched a lot of TV and, because I was in the unworthiness cycle, advertising had a detrimental impact on me. Maybe you remember an ad in the 1970s for Enjoli perfume. A woman sang, "I can bring home the bacon, fry it up in a pan and never let you forget you're a man. I can work until five o'clock. Come home and read your tickety tock. And if it is love that you want, I can kiss you and give you the shivers." The male voiceover then said, "Enjoli: the eight-hour perfume for your twenty-four hour woman."

While I didn't run out to buy the perfume, I did glean from the ad that I could have a career, family, gourmet meals on the table, and hot sex—and it would be a piece of cake. Things were changing for women and more opportunities were available when I graduated from college. I happily set out to be the Enjoli woman—with the corporate job, the fantastic dinners, and all that great sex. No one told me I might be too tired at the end of a sixteen-hour workday to manage even one of those things. Once I started climbing the corporate ladder, I realized that I was going to have to kill myself to make my Enjoli dream a reality. And by ignoring how exhausted I was at the end of every day, I just about did. Being that woman was how I would prove my worth. I had to be her.

There is no product in the world that can increase or decrease your sense of worth. But we continually forget this. Watch TV with your kids for ten minutes, and you'll see how quickly they can misconstrue where worthiness comes from—from cereal to candy to toy ads. And how easy it is to train their minds to look for it outside themselves and start the cycle of unworthiness.

How many times have you purchased a product or a program thinking, *This* is the answer to my problems and once I slather this product on or complete this course, I will be _____ (fill in the blank: beautiful/smart/ready) and life will be perfect? I'm right there with you. None of the products I've purchased over the years made me feel better about myself and all the programs with all the promises never resolved my basic dilemma. In fact, I never even started many of the programs—they sat on my shelf collecting dust. Now before I purchase one, I ask myself, "Is there something in this program I can learn that will enhance my mind and do I have time to take on one more thing right now?" If the reason I am buying it is because I think I need it to improve my worthiness factor or it will make me happy, I don't buy it. I have also come to the conclusion that the people who say they've got one simple formula to solve your problem have lost touch with reality. There is never one formula that works for everyone. It's like the one size fits all clothing— no such thing.

Back to my Enjoli problem. When I was young, my sisters, friends, or parents told me it was impossible to have both a career *and* a family. My mother was a stay at home mom until I was in my teens and then she finished her college education and started a career in a corporation. She worked eight to five, Monday through Friday, which left my little sister and me "latchkey kids." I remember coming home and wanting to chat with my mom about the school day and the questions I had about life, but she was not there. By the time she got home from work, I had long forgotten my questions and my day, so the conversations never happened. I instead searched for answers in advertising, TV shows, novels, and, of course, with my girlfriends who probably understood as little about life as I did. Raised with those distorted views and opinions, it's no wonder I thought I could make the Enjoli life work. I could climb the corporate ladder, have the family, and the hot sex, and I was going to prove everyone who said I couldn't do it wrong.

That thinking nearly cost me my life. I was diagnosed with adrenal fatigue after my layoff. The adrenal glands release hormones that are essential for you to live. When your adrenals are not working properly it can lead to serious dis-ease or illness in other parts of your body. I feel like the loss of my job saved me from a serious illness that I could have gotten had I not stopped working too many hours each week. It made me stop, rest, rejuvenate, and heal my body before it became a life-threatening illness. I also realized that the way I was doing my job was sucking the life right out of me. I see huge perfection in that now. I am grateful for the loss of my job for that very reason. I am also grateful because it brought me back home to my family and opened up my eyes to what I was missing by working non-stop.

I can see clearly how my deep sense of unworthiness led me to work too much and eventually burnout. I worked like that to prove to everyone that it was possible and because the ads said it was true. I did it to prove I was worthy of having it all and worthy of taking up space on our planet.

You may be wondering why I didn't question the messages I was getting. As young, impressionable adults, we want to fit in. We want to belong and end up looking in all the wrong places to find the answers. Unfortunately, advertising is directed at young people. Unless someone is there to help them sort out and question the messages, they easily believe them.

Being trained to look for worthiness outside yourself starts early, comes from many directions, and gets installed into your subconscious mind. Eventually these thoughts start to run your life automatically.

Let's look at how you learn unworthiness in more detail.

You Seek Outside Validation

As I mentioned earlier, your parents may withhold love and approval when you are less than perfect. Growing up in an abusive home, I thought that if I was perfect my parents would love and approve of me and abuse me less. I wanted to be worthy of their love and approval. This conditioned me to change the way I acted, responded, and left me always looking for my approval and worthiness outside myself. I became a doormat of sorts putting everyone else's needs before my own in hopes that they would see how worthy I was and would love me more.

Abused children generally have little to no self-worth or self-love and think they are not loveable unless they are pleasing others. And that feeling can last a lifetime. At my job, even if I already had more work than I could handle, I would always volunteer for more. I thought this made me worthier to the corporation. It actually did the opposite because well before I hit burnout, my creativity and productivity tanked—making me much less of an asset.

The problem with looking outside yourself for your worthiness is, if that outside influence goes away, it takes your worthiness with it. When the company I worked so hard for invited me to leave, I woke up the day after my departure with no self-belief, no self-worth, and no self-love. They were all sitting back at the desk I left the day before and I felt like I was *nothing* without my role at work. Now *that* is a wakeup call.

You're Told to Be the Best

Growing up did you hear your parents tell you to strive to be the best at everything? Be the best in your class. Be the best on your sports team. Be the best in your school. Be the best in your dance class. Be the best and then you will be worthy, happy, and lovable.

But what happens when you are not the best? Does that make you unworthy? If you are using "Be the Best" as your measuring stick, then yes, you will be less worthy if you are second or tenth in your class. Being the best at something is attaching your worthiness to an external force. If the something shifts and your position changes, your worthiness is going to take a hit.

You Hear "No, No, No" Too Often

Your parents told you "NO" hundreds of times a day. According to experts, the average one-year-old hears "NO" more than 400 times per day[2]. You may be thinking there is no way you say it that much. But think about it. When you need to stop your child, do you say it once or multiple times? Most people repeat the word several times at each occurrence of behavior they want to discourage. Sometimes it comes with a slap on the hand or the behind.

While this response might prevent a certain behavior, it quickly teaches a child to behave in a way that

---

[2] www.redbookmag.com/life/mom-kids/advice/a2560/how-to-say-no/

pleases their parent so they don't get slapped, spanked, or yelled at. Children want their parents' approval; even the abused child seeks approval and acceptance from an abusive parent. It is an innate instinct of human nature. When you don't receive that unconditional approval from your parents you become disappointed, feel unlovable, and unworthy.

Your Religion Limits You

Organized religion will have you believe that if you sin you are not worthy of heaven. I am not here to discuss whether there are Pearly Gates and Judgment Day. I'd rather believe that God is unconditional love and expects you to make mistakes and learn and grow from them—and that God forgives you faster than you forgive yourself.

As a child, I had friends from a variety of religions and found it interesting to learn how differently each church deciphered the doctrine. The stricter the religion my friends belonged to, the more fearful of life they were. Some of them were afraid to take a tiny step off the beaten path for fear that God would strike them down on the spot.

Can you imagine waiting until judgement day to find out if you lived a worthy life?

Can people raised in such a fearful religious background ever feel worthy?

Installed Messages

Like it or not, you had messages installed into you. Some empowered you ("You've got this, sweetheart!" or "You know what to do, son") and some of them are still holding you back and negatively affecting your life. Some you may not even know about because they have been comfortably sitting in your subconscious just running your life without you realizing it.

Another version of the "life is hard" message that my parents drilled into me was "nothing in life worth having comes easy." I also took that to mean that I was not worthy of whatever goodness came my way if it came to me easily. Early on, I was a fearless, happy-go-lucky girl with lots of tomboy in me. I could climb trees with the best of them. If my parents were right, all these things that came easy—friends, good grades, and sports— I didn't really deserve and was not worthy of having.

This message is part of what drove me to be such a workaholic during my corporate career. My logic: If my climb up the corporate ladder is easy, it's *not* worth having. So I made that climb up the ladder more difficult than it had to be to prove I was worthy of the success I was creating. This left me exhausted, angry, resentful, and nothing I ever did ever felt good enough.

School

Those years of junior high (middle school) have got to be the cruelest time in school. You are moving from childhood into adulthood, letting go of innocence, and entering into responsibility. Your body is changing. You are trying to find your way and fit in. Trying to be true to yourself but not really sure who you really are yet. Bombarded with so many messages from teachers, coaches, parents, friends, and other teens in the same boat. Unsure whether to fit in with the "cool" kids, be yourself, or find your own group of friends and hang in that safety zone?

It is during this time of life that you can easily lose "yourself" because you listen to others and leave what you *think* is your truth to set out on a slippery slope of trying to fit in, but not really feeling comfortable there. The thing is, the "cool" kids don't feel comfortable in their skin either. They just pretend they do. They are really just showing the façade they think the world is expecting from them.

Take the jock athlete who helps win the game each week. His classmates put him up on a pedestal and he feels he needs to return back what his classmates have given him. Each week he's got to perform or his classmates will take down his pedestal. That's a lot of pressure and his worthiness depends on it.

Then there's the smartest kid in the class. Everyone makes fun of her, but secretly wishes they could get her good grades. The class Brainiac pretends the constant taunting doesn't bother her, but yearns to be one of the "cool" kids. Everyone is wanting to be somebody else because there is no comfort in your own skin at this age.

Open communication with parents is so important during this time because they can help you work through all of this. Unfortunately, parents often check out at this point because they think they don't know the answers or remember it being awful and think that is the way it is supposed to be. They rationalize that any pressure their child goes through builds character. Teens don't usually want to turn to their parents because they think they will not understand. They don't realize that their parents went through the same horrible time in their life, too.

Think back to those years. What would have made

them more bearable? Unconditionally loving parents who asked questions and listened to what you were dealing with daily would have helped. They could ease this painful transition from childhood to adult so you could come out the other end with more confidence, worthiness, and authenticity.

Instead you quickly learn what façade to show the world so you fit in. You create an uncomfortable comfort zone. You know what to do so you don't get tortured or bullied which creates your comfort zone. It denies you of what and who you are which makes it uncomfortable because you are trying to be someone you are not.

By the time you enter high school, you've perfected the façade—and then you enter adulthood conflicted because you have let others determine your place and denied yourself and the world your own greatness. You have dimmed your worthiness light.

So many subconscious messages now run your life without you even knowing it. Messages like:

- I am unworthy unless I hide the real me from the world and pretend I am just like everyone else.
- I am unworthy of huge success unless I play

their game.
- I am unlovable unless I go along with what others say.
- I am "not good enough" unless I am perfect.
- I am uncool unless I get drunk like everyone else.
- I am uncool unless I break my parent's rules like the "cool" kids.

When you're run by these messages, you don't know that you have creative powers to create the life you were put on this earth to live. You can't see your magnificence. The one thing you know is how to fit in because you learned it really well.

Here's an example: When I was young I started piano lessons and added flute lessons when I was older. I was really good at both. In junior high, I hid these accomplishments from my classmates because I did not want to be made fun of. I did not tell anyone that I went to competitions on the weekends and won first place. I kept my lessons and prizes secret for fear that others would not accept me.

You're Overloaded with Information

While all the available technology can promote productivity, it can also repeatedly impact your worthiness. If you are looking for proof that you are indeed unworthy, you can find it on the internet any time of day and not have time to process, sort, or discern it. Being bombarded with information so quickly works like negative affirmations. If you hear them enough times you start to believe them.

Before the internet, people used the library for research. They watched news once a day in the evening, not 24-7. Now, there is information coming at us from the moment we wake to our last glance at our Smart Phone before sleeping. Information overload is costing corporations $900 billion dollars a year in lost productivity and creativity[3]. And it's costing you, too, by depleting your worthiness with rapid-fire messages telling you that you are not enough.

We even have an annual Information Overload day now in late October[4]. It's helpful that we can joke about it. I love this New Yorker cartoon by David Sipress that, ironically, went viral on social media.

---

[3] https://hbr.org/2009/09/death-by-information-overload

[4] https://www.daysoftheyear.com/days/information-overload-day

My desire to be well-informed is currently at odds with my desire to remain sane.

SUMMARY

You were born with an unlimited supply of worthiness. Then you were taught to view yourself as unworthy and started being bombarded with proof that you are not enough. When you hear this enough, you begin to believe it. When you look outside yourself for your self-worth, you give your power away to people, things, and events that are probably not accurate reflections of who you are.

Whenever I start questioning my own worth, I tell myself, "Never give your power away to someone that may be more confused and tormented than you."

You have choices. You can choose to be your own best friend or your worst enemy. You can choose to love yourself, flaws and all, or use those flaws to tell yourself that you are unlovable and unworthy. You learned unworthiness and you can unlearn it.

Chapter Two: The Unworthiness Cycle

Being stuck in the unworthiness cycle is defeating and frustrating. You start out with high hopes that *this* time things will turn out differently. But if you never do things differently you always get the same result. You have probably heard insanity defined as doing the same thing over and over and expecting different results. The *only* way to get different results is to do something different than you normally do: Step outside your uncomfortable comfort zone and take a different path.

Portia Nelson's poem titled "Autobiography in 5 Chapters" says it perfectly.

I
I walk down the street.
There is a deep hole in the sidewalk
I fall in.
I am lost...
I am hopeless.
It isn't my fault.
It takes forever to find a way out.

II
I walk down the same street.
There is a deep hole in the sidewalk.

I pretend I don't see it.
I fall in again.
I can't believe I'm in the same place.
But it isn't my fault.
It still takes a long time to get out.

III
I walk down the same street.
There is a deep hole in the sidewalk.
I see it is there.
I still fall in... It's a habit
My eyes are open; I know where I am;
It is my fault.
I get out immediately.

IV
I walk down the same street.
There is a deep hole in the sidewalk.
I walk around it.

V
I walk down another street.

I love how this poem so clearly defines how to move outside a cycle that is not serving you. And it's exactly what happens in the unworthiness cycle. Your first reaction is to blame others. To break out of the cycle, you must take responsibility for your actions, conscious of what you are doing and creating. Once you are conscious you can make different choices to step outside the cycle of unworthiness and into a cycle of worthiness.

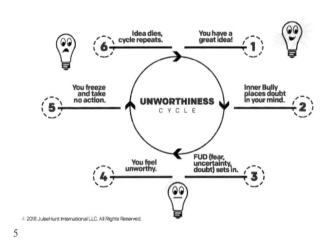

5

Here's how it goes. The unworthiness cycle always starts with a great idea, or a light bulb moment. You get excited about it. Let's say your idea is to start an exercise program. This will make you feel better, give you more energy, and is good for your health. You make a plan to start by going to the gym before work five days a week.

---

5 Graphic by Jenna Balogh www.jennabalogh.com

Day One: You set your alarm earlier than normal so you can hit the gym nice and early. The night before you packed everything you need so you can go directly to the office from the gym. The alarm goes off and because you are excited about your great idea, you hop out of bed, grab your bag, and off you go to the gym. Afterward you feel proud of yourself for implementing the new idea. This time you will see it through.

Day Two: The alarm goes off early again. You get up with a little less enthusiasm, but you made a commitment so you grab your bag and off to the gym you go. Afterward you feel energetic and happy. You are so glad you got up even though you were tired when you heard the alarm. You vow to go to bed earlier to avoid that feeling tomorrow.

Day Three: The alarm goes off early. You are tired because you did not go to bed earlier the night before even though you said you would. You slowly get out of bed, wearily pick up your bag and head to the gym. In the car on the way to work you wonder if you can keep up this intense early morning schedule. FUD begins to penetrate your thoughts. You start to question whether you are worthy of this great idea.

Day Four: The alarm goes off early. This time you

hit the snooze button once. You get up ten minutes later, then realize you did not pack your bag the night before and are even later. Your Inner Bully ignites. You berate yourself for not being organized and hitting the snooze button. You quickly pack a bag and make it to the gym for a shorter work out.

Your Inner Bully plants the seed in your head that this work out idea may not be so good after all. Afterward you feel tired instead of energetic. Your Inner Bully has made you feel defeated. As you are getting dressed for work in the locker room, you realize you have on two different color shoes.

You head home to fix your shoe faux pas. Now you are late for work *and* stuck in traffic. This is clearly not working. Your Inner Bully is reminding you that your great ideas never work and why do you even try? In the end, you always fail. You decide you will try again tomorrow despite the FUD that your Inner Bully has stirred up.

Day Five: The alarm goes off. Even though you are exhausted you decide to get up and hope you will have a different result than yesterday. It is hard enough to get out to the car, much less lift the weights. Your Inner Bully starts in again with the negative self-talk. You finish the workout and head to work. On the way, you wonder what you were thinking on Monday anyway. Why did you think you could start an exercise plan when you never finish anything?

This constant bullying continues throughout the day. By the time you get home, you feel like a limp noodle. You have successfully convinced yourself that you are unworthy of the many benefits the exercise program will bring you. You decide to abandon it. You rationalize that you need the extra sleep more. On Sunday night, you set your alarm for your original time and skip the gym.

Week Two: Your Inner Bully is going berserk, reminding you that you've failed once again. You feel unworthy of ever being able to complete a great idea. You put yourself back in your place of unworthiness—your uncomfortable comfort zone— because you know how things go there. You don't know how they will turn out if you actually bring a great idea to fruition and that has your Inner Bully freaked out. By the end of the week, you are back to where you started, letting your Inner Bully run the show and feeling like a failure, unworthy of success.

This cycle is uncomfortable and keeps you stuck in the same place. Eventually, you feel so bad about yourself for failing, you vow never to try again. As time passes, however, you start to believe maybe you *could* succeed if you tried once more. The problem is that you've never learned how to silence your Inner Bully and once she's spoken, it's all over.

It is only by silencing her that you get a different result. This requires stepping outside your uncomfortable comfort zone and into the unknown to create a *new* comfort zone, one in which you discover you ARE worthy.

What Triggers Your Unworthiness?

You can identify when you are in the unworthiness cycle by paying attention to the triggers that put you there.

These can look like:

- Blaming others
- Feeling guilty or hurt
- Getting irritated by others' behaviors
- Listening to your Inner Bully
- Letting perfectionism take a front seat in your life
- Resistance

When I was stuck in a soul-sucking job and life (and endlessly circling the cycle of unworthiness), I blamed everyone else for the miserable life I was living. I blamed my abusive parents for not empowering me to believe in myself. I blamed bosses for not seeing what a good employee I was. I blamed friends for making me think I was not enough. I blamed my husband for making me think I was unlovable.

I took no responsibility for my miserable life. I actually believed that if only everyone would get on my bandwagon and do it my way, my life would be awesome, amazing, and I would finally feel worthy.

Today I know I'm entering the cycle when I feel agitated, fearful, resistance, or unhappy, and start looking outside myself for the source of these feelings. I know I'm there anytime I start playing the "When I" game. (When I get past this project, I will be happy again. When I get more sleep, I will be happy again. When I get my husband to see how important it is that I work like a dog, I will be happy again.) Or I look at other people and start picking them apart for everything they're doing wrong or imperfectly. I focus on the negative and let everything outside myself rule my mood and attitude.

These triggers let me know I am in the unworthiness cycle and to get out, I must do something different.

Here's an example: It used to send me over the edge when people were late for appointments. We'd decide on a day to meet, set a time and place, and I would arrive early and wait. When the meeting time came and went I would start getting irritated. I would use their lateness as proof that I was unlovable, unimportant, and unworthy. I would let my Inner Bully tell me, "See, no one sees you as important as you see them. No one cares as much as you do. Why do you even bother trying to have friends? They just disappoint you over and over again." It kept me firmly stuck in the cycle of unworthiness.

Then I attended a weekend Shadow Work retreat where we were asked to write down something that irritated us on a regular basis. Shadow Work involves looking at those parts of yourself that you have disowned because you think they are bad or unbecoming. I wrote, "I hate when people are late to meet me."

The facilitator asked us to look at where this behavior showed up in our own lives. I thought, "Is she crazy? I am never late."

That, my friend, is called resistance and is one of those things we use to dig our heels into the ground and refuse to listen, grow, or change.

She asked me to scour my life and see where I was late. Turns out, I was often late to pick up or meet my husband—the one person who loved and supported me. He is a very flexible person so it never bothered him, but it bothered me when I was late. By the time I arrived, I had berated myself so badly for not leaving earlier, I was a hot mess of self-loathing. I was treating the most important person in my life with disrespect and making him unimportant by being late to meet him or pick him up. When I realized this, I vowed to leave earlier when it came to meeting my husband.

I did not see this cycle when I was in it, but when I got some distance, it was obvious. And I learned that anytime someone irritates me, it is a sign to look within and see where I have this behavior.

Life gives us ample opportunities to catch those triggers in action. Here's one of my doozies. A few years ago, I decided to run a half-marathon. I followed the training plan to the T and I was sure that I could finish that race in two and a half hours or less. At mile six, I felt a sharp pain in my gut. At first, I thought it was a side ache and if I just kept running it would go away. Eventually it got so bad I almost gave up. I must have looked a bit gray because one of the race monitors stopped and asked me if I was OK. If he'd had a car with him I might have jumped in, but he was on a bike, so I said, "I'm good."

I walked for a while and then the first marathoner ran by me. You know, the ones who run twenty-six miles? Mind you, they left a good twenty minutes before me and ran twice as far. I remember thinking, "Oh hell no, I am not going to come in after a marathoner." I started running again, but the pain was too great. I had to walk and run the last three miles and I crossed the finish line at three hours. I felt defeated, like I let myself down. I actually felt unworthy of the amazing medal they shoved in my hand as I crossed the finish line.

I spent the next three days letting my Inner Bully tear me down and abuse me. Because my time was thirty minutes longer than my goal, I felt my race was not perfect and I was unworthy of the medal and the accomplishment.

Wow, right?

I finished a half-marathon! No matter what the time, wouldn't you say that is worthy of a medal? Not for me back then. And that pain I experienced for more than half the race? It was a _hernia_. The following week I had surgery. It would be a long while before I let go of that kind of perfectionism, but today I know that whenever I let my Inner Bully abuse me like this, I'm stuck in the cycle of unworthiness.

Another trigger for me was my long list of "shitty shoulds" that kept me circling the unworthiness cycle on a continuous basis. These are the things you do because you _should_ rather than because you _want_ to, e.g. I should have run the race in two and a half hours. I let this "should" take away my accomplishment and make me feel unworthy of the achievement. Holy cow, I ran 13.1 miles—that's friggin' awesome!

Holidays are often filled with "shitty shoulds," which can make them disappointing and exhausting. When my husband and I were newly married we tried to make the whole family happy by stopping by everyone's house over the holidays. This meant visiting my mother, my father, my in-laws, and my sisters—all because we believed we *should*. The logistics alone were a living nightmare, not to mention that each one of them wanted us to eat at their house. I ate a little at each house to be polite. After all, they spent hours preparing the holiday meal. You might say I "should" all over myself.

At the end of the day, we were exhausted from driving, miserable because we ate too much, and glad the day was over and that we would not have to do it again until the next holiday. Sound like a day you want to experience on a regular basis? Me, neither.

How many "shitty shoulds" do you have in your life? One of my teachers taught me to remove the word "should" from my vocabulary and replace it with "could." I tried it on and I love it. I *could* go to everyone's house for the holiday or I *could* pick one and enjoy the day.

Could is filled with possibility. *Should* reeks of shame, guilt, and anxiety. The rigid and inflexible "shitty shoulds" keep you stuck in the unworthiness cycle.

You may see where you tend to get stuck in the cycle—and notice the triggers that alert you to when you're getting close to entering. Take heart! It's totally possible to become self-aware enough that you catch yourself and don't enter it anymore. In the next section, you'll learn about the Worthiness Cycle, a much more fun and rewarding place to hang out.

SUMMARY

The unworthiness cycle is an uncomfortable comfort zone and unless you are willing to step outside it and do something different when your Inner Bully places doubt in your mind, you stay stuck here. You can break the cycle by learning how to silence your Inner Bully and giving her a new role. Shadow work will help to identify your unworthiness cycle. This lets you know what your triggers are and how to identify them, so the next time it happens you can choose to step outside the cycle and create a different result.

Chapter Three: Symptoms of Unworthiness

I kept secrets much of my adult life. My co-workers had no idea how unhappy I was or that my marriage was on the rocks. Pretending to be someone I wasn't sucked. Denying my magnificence was a horrible way to live. I was not only denying myself, but I was withholding my gifts and talents from the world. I was totally stuck in the unworthiness cycle.

Unworthiness has many symptoms that show up in your life and hold you back from the life you desire. Not only the life you desire, but that next promotion, or finding your soulmate, or truly feeling happy. The kicker is you may not even know you are feeling unworthy because you have learned to play the game of life according to someone else's rules. You're no longer in touch with yourself – what you like, how you feel, your own thoughts. You're inauthentic. You are obsessed with what other people think you should say, do, or be. It is called denial of self.

As far back as I can remember—back to when I first saw those Enjoli "bring home the bacon" ads in the 1970s— I wanted to climb the corporate ladder and be the CEO of a company. I knew that CEOs made tons of money, traveled the world, and contributed to the betterment of society. It sounded like noble work. And I knew that if I worked hard, studied hard, made good grades, and stayed focused, I could make my dream come true. That's what I'd been taught and I believed it. I aced my way through school and landed a sweet job at an international software company. I began my climb to the top, certain I'd achieve the title of CEO.

Twenty-five years into my career, and a few rungs away from that coveted status, 9/11 happened. Business came to a screeching halt. I went from traveling weekly to once every three months. After several months of this scenario, with profits dwindling and a dismal bottom line, our company had to make some tough decisions.

One morning, I received a call from my boss. She told me I had to lay off my *entire* North American team. These were people I had hand-picked and were top performers. They were also friends. I sat down and sobbed. One by one I called each one to deliver the bad news. Each time I hung up the phone, the knot in my stomach got tighter and tighter. After I finished laying each one off—one of the hardest things I've ever done, I hesitantly contacted my boss and asked, "Now what?" praying she was not going to lay me off.

She didn't, but that didn't mean all was well. My unworthiness, along with my anxiety, was kicked up a few notches. For an entire year I traveled at a moment's notice anywhere they needed me. I could be in Seattle one day and New York the next. My constant thought was, "Work harder, work longer hours, or you, too, could lose your job."

Did you catch that? "You, too, could lose your job." My thoughts actually made the decision about whether or not I'd stay at my job, and I didn't realize what I was doing. No surprise that one year later I was invited to leave my job.

I packed my things and left in shock, with a very active Inner Bully going nuts in my mind. The next day I woke up feeling devastated and lost. And realized that my self-worth, self-love, self-belief, and identity were still sitting at the desk I left the day before. Ouch!

There are many symptoms associated with the unworthiness cycle. These are the ten most prevalent and common ones. If you start to see yourself in this list, it is not an invitation to berate yourself. It is an invitation to notice, learn, and grow. An invitation to return to your true authentic self.

You Play Small

Playing small means you live in fear of being seen. You want to stay invisible because you don't feel your contribution to the world is significant enough to be seen. One woman told me when she and her husband would go to parties with his co-workers, she would find a tall plant in the room and hide behind it. At the end of the evening he would come fetch her from her hiding spot and they would go home. I asked her why she did this. She said, "These people all have big, important careers and I'm just a housewife." She wanted to stay invisible. I asked her these questions:

- Are you running a household while your husband goes to work each day?
- Are you raising the future generation that will be shaping the future of our country?
- Do you manage several people and multiple schedules just like a manager in a corporation?
- Are you aware that being a housewife is a career and is a "big, important job"?

"Well, when you say it like that it does sound important," she said. Changing her perspective on her role in the world and how it compared to others made her realize that being a stay-at-home mom is a big, important job. She no longer needed to be invisible.

You're a Negative Nelly

When you are stuck in the unworthiness cycle your attitude, well, stinks. The glass is always half empty. You judge others and repel goodness. Even when good things come your way, you are always waiting for the other shoe to drop. You rarely smile or laugh. You have trouble seeing possibilities. You are the naysayer at work and home. You're easily overwhelmed. You feel hopeless and dejected regularly.

Think about the people you work with or spend time with. Are any of them negative? How do you feel after you spend time with them? Do they zap your mood? Do they bring your energy down? Do you get frustrated with their constant naysaying? Positive people rarely want to spend time with negative people because they put a damper on every situation—they're not only exhausted; they're exhausting.

When Negative Nelly feeds your mind stinkin'

thinkin' and negative self-talk, it sounds like this:

- I'm unworthy of huge success.
- I'm unlovable unless I am perfect.
- The likeliness of huge success is doubtful because I am dumb.
- I will be happy when I get the next promotion at work.
- I'm ugly.
- I'm too fat.

Your Negative Nelly is an Inner Bully. She thinks she is trying to protect you from the big bad world. In reality, she lives in a constant state of fear and is holding you back. She is a liar, a terrorist, and verbally abusive. She keeps you stuck in one place out of fear that if you move from that spot something bad will happen. She brainwashes you into believing you are not enough. The question to ask yourself when you listen to her is, "Would I let my best friend talk to me this way?"

No, of course not. Then why would you talk to yourself that way?

You're Depressed

If you are living the unworthiness cycle, depression is

your constant companion. Depression is at such a high level in our society, that hundreds of pharmaceutical companies are racing to create drugs to combat it. If you could eliminate your unworthiness by changing your thoughts and focus, you likely wouldn't need drugs. Now, some people have chemical imbalances and require these drugs to combat the depression. But the sheer number of people on these drugs is overwhelming. This number would shrink if we could teach people to see, acknowledge, and honor their worthiness.

According to the Centers for Disease Control, antidepressant use increased sixty-five percent over a fifteen year time frame from 1999 to 2014. During 2011-2014 about one in eight Americans aged twelve and over reported taking antidepressants in the previous month.[6] Global revenue for antidepressants was about $14.5 billion in 2014 and is projected to grow to nearly $17 billion over the next three years.[7]

In my late thirties, after having my son, I suffered from postpartum depression. It was horrible. I cried every day and could not understand why I was so sad when I had the beautiful baby I wanted. In my heart,

---

[6] https://www.cdc.gov/richs/products/databriefs/db283.htm

[7] http://time.com/4876098/new-hope-for-depression/

I felt like I had created this familial panacea, but my mind was depressed and unhappy. I was told that this could last a few days, weeks, or even months. After an entire year of depression, I was told that in extreme cases it may take up to three years. I eventually went on one of the depression drugs and I felt like a zombie, a lifeless shell—unhappy, unfulfilled, and empty. I questioned being on the drug and how addictive it might be, knowing that I'd eventually have to be weaned off of it.

I remember trying two or three different prescriptions, all with the same Zombie effect. I did not end up weaning myself off, I quit cold turkey knowing deep in my soul that this was not my answer. I later learned that I was very low on progesterone and as soon as I started using a bioidentical progesterone cream, my depression went away overnight. I was one of those people who definitely did not need to be on any of the depression drugs, but I did have a hormonal imbalance.

When I look back at that time in my life, I can see that I felt unworthy of this happy family I had created. I was repelling the goodness that had come my way in order to stay in the unworthiness cycle. If I had had the tools to move from unworthy to worthy, from lack of belief to belief in myself, would I have been able to turn the depression around without drugs or hormones? Perhaps my low hormone levels were caused by my negative mindset? I am sure the depression drugs were not my answer and know for a fact that it was a misdiagnosis. How many other people are on these drugs unnecessarily? And why aren't we teaching people how to feel better without them?

The mind is a powerful thing. When you feel unworthy you can actually upset the chemical balance in your body. Depression can change your whole physiology. Plus, it keeps you from being happy, from having a divine relationship, and from attracting abundance into your life. Negative thoughts can lead to depression, weaken you physically, and attack your muscles, including your heart. As a result, negative thoughts can shorten your life, age you more quickly, and break down the molecular structure of your body. How would you feel if you knew that changing your thoughts could improve or eliminate the chemical imbalance in your body without prescription drugs?

You Look Outside Yourself for Validation

How much power do you give to the outside world and to things you have little to no control over? When you are unworthy, you look for validation and approval outside yourself.

You compare yourself to others and you never quite measure up. You find yourself wishing you could be just like someone else or living someone else's life. You really don't know what they're dealing with beneath the façade they share with the world. But when you look at them you are sure they have the perfect life and you want it, too.

On social media, where everyone shares only their best and most beautiful stuff with the public, it is so easy to compare and put others on a pedestal. When you do this, you give away your power. You let other people determine your self-worth. People who in reality may feel even less worthy than you. Maybe you attach your worthiness to a job or a spouse. What happens if the job or spouse go away? They take your worthiness with them and you are stuck trying to find another job or spouse to fill your worthiness void. When I got laid off from the job I'd attached my worthiness to it was all gone. I was overwhelmed at the thought of starting all over proving my worthiness somewhere else.

When you look outside yourself for your worthiness, you expect the world to bring you happiness, love, joy, and everything you desire. You don't have confidence in who you are and what you can create by being you. Self-confidence is believing in your own abilities and judgements. When you don't have it, you give other people the right to make your decisions. You ask multiple people, even strangers, what they think or what they would do. Eventually you have too many options in front of you and still don't know which one is right. Overwhelmed, you throw your hands in the air and don't make a decision. It is a frustrating and exhausting cycle.

In my "practice marriage" I put *all* my worth outside myself. I could not wait to start married life so I could prove I was worthy of happiness. I married at twenty-one, to a man seven years older, while pursuing a degree in education. I envisioned being a teacher so I could be home with my children in the summer and I thought finally, the world would value me.

On my wedding day, I knew I was making a mistake, but it was too late. After all, 350 people were sitting in the park waiting for the ceremony to begin. How could I let them down? The signs were everywhere, the biggest of all was that I did not want to be there, at my own wedding. I felt sick walking down the aisle with my father when all I wanted to do was turn around and run the other way. Our expensive wedding cake with Bavarian cream filling slid down the table layer by layer due to the scorching heat. We argued as we drove to our honeymoon destination. On our honeymoon, I was up early ready to go adventuring for the day and had no desire to lie in marital bliss with my new husband. I ended up cutting our trip short.

Because I did not feel worthy of love or happiness (and went through with the wedding because I was afraid what people would think if I didn't), I sabotaged that marriage from Day One. It turns out we were incompatible, with verbal and occasional physical abuse on both sides. I am grateful I had the courage to leave within three years. It took me a lot more years to learn how to finally love myself and find my worth inside.

You have the choice to listen to what others say or not. A mentor of mine once told me that other people's opinions of me are none of my business. I used to take what others said—or might say—to heart. Sometimes it hurt. I would change who I was and pretend to be someone else (even walking down the aisle) to gain their love and approval. What I realized is that they rarely noticed because they were stuck in their own unworthiness story and could not even see that I had changed. Never give your worthiness away to someone more messed up than you!

***

When my son was eight, my mother visited from out of town. He had been outside playing most of the day and asked if he could watch some TV. He sprawled out on the couch and started watching one of his favorite programs. I was in the kitchen making dinner when I heard my mother say to him, "You know, no one will marry you if you are lazy."

My chopping went from steady to feverish. The hair on the back of my neck stood up and I wanted to run in there and scream at her that she may have been verbally abusive to me, but she could not do the same to my child. I held myself back. I never wanted to be one of those moms that was always rescuing her child—I wanted to empower him to do that for himself. I waited to see what was going to happen.

Before I knew it, he was by my side whispering to me, asking me if I had heard what Grandma said. I looked at him and said, "I did. Do you believe what she said about you? Do you feel like you are lazy?"

He said, "You always tell me to check in with my tummy to see if what other people say about me feels like it is true to me. My tummy says it is not true and I do not believe I am lazy."

"And what do you do when someone says something

about you that is not your truth?" I asked.

He said, "I let it roll off my back like water rolls off a duck's back."

I gave him a hug and he skipped off with a smile on his face. It was priceless. I knew right then and there that our parenting techniques were working and he was going to grow up with his worthiness intact—and his sense of self-worth coming from inside. He would start adulthood much differently than I had and that made my heart sing.

You're an Expert at the "When I…" Game

When you are circling around the unworthiness cycle, you typically play the "When I…" Game, which I described earlier.

You decide that you will be happy when you…

- lose ten pounds.
- promote to the next level.
- make more money.
- get married.
- take a vacation to an exotic locale.
- have a baby.
- get divorced.

You get the idea. You will be happy when a certain event occurs. This is also giving the power of your happiness to external sources—and setting up very specific conditions for that happiness. Here's what I've noticed: When you actually achieve your "When I…," your happiness is temporary and pretty soon it dissipates because you start picking it apart. You start thinking about the next thing that will make you happy and attach your happiness to another event. You become to happiness what a dog is to his tail, chasing it endlessly and never catching it.

After my practice marriage ended, I vowed to never marry again. Imagine my surprise when Prince Charming came to work at the same company as me.

My second marriage, to a man who swept me off my feet at the job I felt like I was married to, temporarily made me very happy. Until I felt my unworthiness rear its ugly head. I could only see what was wrong with him instead of all the things that were right. I second-guessed my decision-making skills in even deciding to marry again. I did not think I was worthy of all this happiness so I started to sabotage it. I would sulk and accuse him of not being unconditionally loving or approving of me. I blamed him for being just like my abusive father. We almost did not make it through our first year of marriage.

All these things I was accusing him of? All were things I was not doing for myself. I was not loving me. I let my Inner Bully abuse me verbally just like my father. I am grateful to say that I grew out of that, and we are nearing our thirtieth anniversary.

Unworthiness repels happiness in your life because you are always waiting for something bad to happen and that's the instruction you're sending out into the ethers of the world. The solution to the "When I…" game is to be those things *now* regardless of external circumstances. Be happy now and then when the event that you thought would make you happy happens, it is icing on the cake. It does not determine your happiness, it just enhances it!

You Attack, Blame, and Criticize (ABC)

In the unworthiness cycle, you want to blame others for the miserable life you are living. You don't want to be responsible for your disastrous life or for feeling as lousy as you do. So many people blame the government, their boss, their in-laws, or their spouse for their depression or unhappiness. "If only my boss would see how valuable I am, my life would be better." "The government and all their idiotic policies have ruined my life. "

You feel bad. You feel like you can't control a situation. You don't see a way out of it. As a result, you attack, blame, and criticize others to build yourself up so you can see yourself in a (slightly) better light. After your tirade, you feel superior or "better than" the person you berated, but it is temporary. Eventually your Inner Bully does the same thing to you and you fall back into your unworthiness abyss.

Ask yourself these questions:

- Do you criticize and degrade other people on a regular basis?
- Are you quick to attack or blame others as a way to prove your own perfection?
- Do you feel more important than other people when you point out all the things they are doing wrong?

If you answered "YES" to even one of these, you are stuck in the unworthiness cycle. You have a need to make others look worse than you so you can feel better about your own miserable life. It is a sad state of affairs—but it doesn't have to be this way.

I used to come home from work and start picking apart the people I worked with, one by one. I told my husband how Susie disrupted the momentum of our meeting by showing up late again or that Carl shared a ridiculous idea that nearly had me falling out of my chair. The thing I didn't yet know was that when you criticize another person you are also criticizing yourself. Not sure you believe this? The next time you say something snarky about someone, pay attention to the energy in your body. I notice that my shoulders slump, my heart feels sad, and I actually feel worse than before. When I got this, my criticizing talk became an indicator for when I was stuck in my story of unworthiness.

Next time you start the ABCs, remember, other people are your mirror. Whatever you are seeing in them resides in you or you would not be able to see it. Whenever I am frustrated with my husband about something, I know it's time to look within. For instance, if I feel like my husband is not hearing me, I can go down this road of criticism and attack trying to get him to hear me. From telling little stories to yelling as though that will make him hear me better. It never works. Remembering that he is my mirror, though, I go within and see where I am not listening in my own life. It might be not listening to myself, my inner wisdom, not listening to him—or all three. And when I start listening to him, he starts hearing me. Amazing.

You're Obsessed with Perfection

I've already talked a lot about this, but the bottom line is, you were born in perfection. Stop trying to be perfect. That box has been checked and cannot be unchecked. The unworthy soul will spend their whole life trying to be perfect and the only thing it does is make you feel like you never measure up.

On my son's fourth birthday, he wanted a Spiderman party. When I was little girl my mom spent hours making "shape cakes" for our birthdays. I always felt loved when she made me a Holly Hobby cake. It took her hours to bake several cakes, cut them into shapes using frosting to hold them together and create a beautiful masterpiece. (Today you can buy a Holly Hobby cake pan!) My mother happened to visit for this particular birthday and I was fretting about how I was going to make a Spiderman cake. I was sure my mom would be able to help me with this. After she unpacked I asked her advice and she surprised me by saying, "Honey, you work full-time and the bakery makes amazing Spiderman cakes—just order one." I was a bit knocked off kilter, but I ordered a Spiderman cake.

The day came. I set the cake on the counter while I busily prepared the rest of the food. My son was curious about the cake but not tall enough to see it, so he tugged on the corner. The cake slid off the counter and onto the floor. Amazingly it landed right side up on the gold cardboard it came on, but one of the corners was messed up. I got so upset and thought the party was ruined because the cake was no longer perfect. In my anger, I hurt my son's feelings. This ignited my Inner Bully and I was circling the unworthiness cycle faster than a Ferrari in a Formula One Grand Prix race.

It always saddens me to think of this story and how one tiny corner of a cake set me off. Trying to be perfect made me tired, cranky, irritable, and hard to live with. I thought if I showed only "perfection" to the outside world then they would be envious of me and want to be me. But I did not even want to be me. Why I thought the world would think more highly of me if I was perfect is almost outside my scope of understanding now, but I know it all comes from not feeling like I was enough. Let go of this notion that perfection makes you appear worthy.

You were born in perfection. Enough said!

Your Boundaries are Leaky

Boundaries are simply limits you set around something. While writing this book, I set boundaries around my writing time. My phone is off. The only thing open on my PC is my word processor. I put a "do not disturb" sign on my door. I mark it on my calendar and do not book over it. I set boundaries around this time because it is important to me. If I did not set these boundaries and tried to write in random nooks and crannies of my day, it would never happen. Trust me. I tried to do this for a couple years and had very few words on the page.

Boundaries are a crucial part of taking care of yourself. When you feel unworthy, the word "boundary" is not in your vocabulary. You may try to set them, but they are likely in pencil and can be trampled over at a moment's notice.

When I was in my unworthy cycle I could plan my day, but if anyone needed something, I would drop everything and tend to their need. (And I mean *anyone*!) I became a doormat for everyone, especially my family. Whether they forgot their lunch or their homework or their workout clothes or needed me to look up a number they left on their dresser or needed twenty-five cupcakes for their classroom, I would be the hero and save the day. I thought that if I did all that for them, they would love me more. Boy, was I wrong.

They did not love me more for putting their needs before my own. Those things had nothing to do with their love for me. I eventually saw that I was not allowing them to be responsible for their own lives—and I was reinforcing that I was not as important as them. My life, desires, and dreams were always on the back burner waiting for the day when no one would need me to put their needs before mine. And that day was never going to come unless I started honoring my own boundaries.

There was a time I would put a writing session on my calendar, yet I would not honor my own boundary. I would find other things to do like clean the house or run errands and blow by my own boundary. This is what I call a "leaky boundary." At the end of the day, I was so disappointed in myself and felt like crap. My Inner Bully would attack me for not meeting my goal and I'd vow to do better tomorrow. And guess what happened tomorrow? This is how the vicious cycle of unworthiness goes.

There's Never Enough

When you're in scarcity mindset, you hold onto

money because you are afraid there is not enough. You hold onto things because if you let them go they may take your worthiness with them. You hold onto relationships that are unhealthy because you are afraid if you let go you won't have any friends and you'll be alone.

What's under all of this is that you don't feel worthy—of love, wealth, or even better things, and you don't trust the natural ebb and flow of life.

Holding on tight to money and other things stops the flow in and out of your life. Do you spend money on other people, but not on yourself? This is proof again that you believe others are more worthy than you. If you find yourself holding on tightly to something, instead of thinking this is just the way you need to be, take a moment to look within and ask yourself why you're clinging. How would it feel to let go? What is the worst that could happen if you no longer had this money, this person, this object?

You're Addicted

If you are battling an addiction, you are having issues with your worthiness. Addiction comes in many forms:

- Food
- Drugs
- Alcohol
- Shopping
- Social media
- Binge watching TV

Anything that is done in excess on a regular basis is an addiction. Addictions arise from trying to fill the many voids created by unworthiness. The "high" helps temporarily, but soon enough, you're back where you began—feeling lost, lonely, and unworthy.

We lived in a 4,000-square-foot home when I was entrenched in my unworthiness cycle. While I don't really like shopping in stores, I am a great online shopper. If I want or need something I have no problem hopping online and having it show up at my door two days later.

Back to our oversized home. I filled that thing to the brim with kitchen gadgets, shoes, and the newest exercise gimmicks in an effort to fill my void of self-worth and to try and make myself happy. I would be happy for a few minutes when a new item would arrive, but the happiness did not last. Then I would have to buy something else to make me feel worthy again. By the time I was finished I had racked up nearly $70,000 of credit card debt—and I still felt unworthy. In fact, owing this amount ignited my itty bitty shitty committee and sent me into a tailspin of self-loathing, criticism, negativity, shame, blame, and guilt. Things cannot make you happy or make you feel worthy. They may be able to enhance how you feel, but only if you have it inside yourself first.

It's pretty simple: When you feel unworthy you will look for things to make you feel worthy. This is how addictions are born and maintained. They are temporary fillers of your voids. They work for a little while but not forever. It is like sand in a funnel. It blocks the funnel opening for a short time and then eventually it filters through and the void is wide open again.

Addiction is a sign to take a step back and figure out what void you are trying to fill. The reason I addictively worked so many hours during my climb up the corporate ladder was to fill my void of worthiness. The reason I filled up all the closets in our house with things was to fill my void of happiness. The reason I bought lavish gifts for people on their birthdays was to fill my void of being lovable. The voids I was trying to fill were many and deep.

Nothing can fill the voids other than changing the way you see yourself. You were born with everything you need. Somewhere along the way you stopped believing that and in the process started looking for external means to fill the voids.

SUMMARY

The list of symptoms for unworthiness could fill the Grand Canyon. It does not matter if you have one or many, everyone spends time in the unworthiness cycle. It would be impossible to escape with the number of messages thrown at you daily that reinforce your unworthiness. By understanding the symptoms you can see how they impact your life. If you don't like the life you are living now, look no further than your own unworthiness cycle. You are just stuck in a story that is keeping you in this cycle. Write a new story and create a new cycle. If I can do it, so can you!

Chapter Four: The High Cost of Unworthiness in Our World

Unworthiness in society is not pretty. When unworthiness goes unchecked, it becomes encoded in the genetic structure of each generation until it becomes the norm. Health is affected, with symptoms ranging from regular colds to debilitating or even life-threatening diseases. People stop taking responsibility for their own lives and instead hand over the reins to the government, their boss, their friends, spouse, or parents—anyone but themselves. There is always someone to blame when things go wrong or life feels miserable—and children learn to blame others watching their parents do the same.

Then, 24-7 news reporting creates feelings of fear, hopelessness, sadness, and lack of control. A society of people who feel they have no control over their own destiny is a society that can be silenced or wiped off the face of the earth. We've seen this happen again and again throughout history and are witnessing much of the same in our world today.

An unworthy society is more susceptible to marketing by companies that want you to believe that you will be whole, perfect, and complete when you buy their product. And feelings of unworthiness have allowed our society to incur massive amounts of credit card debt, which makes us feel even more unworthy.

Even children who grow up in a loving home that empowers them to walk in their worthiness, can enter the unworthiness cycle thanks to the messages they receive from peers, advertising, and social media.

While it is possible to exit the unworthiness cycle (I'll show you how in the next section), individuals who stay in the cycle of unworthiness are more susceptible to burnout, disease (dis-ease), rote living, unhappiness, and unfulfilling lives.

That's what happened to me.

As I've mentioned, I spent twenty-five years carefully building my career and with one two-minute phone call was cast aside like a stone kicked down the street. I became negative, lost my identity, and my self-confidence sunk to an all-time low. How could I give my life to the Corporation and then be tossed out like garbage? As an over-performer, I'd felt sure that working sixty to eighty hours a week would keep me employed and keep my star on the rise. While the misery felt like it started with my layoff, I had been living a life of quiet desperation long before I lost my job. I felt I had no choice but to work, work, work, and work some more.

The moment I left my job, I lost not only my identity and confidence but also my worthiness, my desire for living, and my dream of reaching the top of the ladder. When I say I had no idea what to do, I mean I did not even *know* what I liked to do—outside of work. I had no real friends and even if I had, I would have been too ashamed to tell them that I lost my job. I had lost the "I" in my life, which left me with what I now call LFE: Life Feels Empty.

The one bright spot was that I was the only mom at the neighborhood pool making a six-figure income while watching my child swim. At least until my severance pay ran out.

Looking back, it is easy to see how distorted my thinking was. The red flags of the unworthiness cycle were waving all around me. Despite having an amazing husband, an awesome son, a warm place to sleep, food on the table, clothes on my back, and more, I felt like I had no reason to live. I was frozen in fear and didn't know how to "do life."

I even went on the Oprah show in 2008 and told

millions of people how lost I felt. Yes, I was on Oprah—but this was NOT one of my finer moments. I cringe to tell you about it today. I would have rather appeared on the show to showcase an amazing accomplishment rather than to describe in detail my feelings of burnout in the unworthiness abyss.

My job loss was my wake-up call. I discovered I had severe adrenal fatigue and was headed for serious illness if I did not stop and tend to my health. I knew that if I did not do something different—and soon—I was going to head right into self-destruction.

It was not until I read an eye-opening article by burnout specialist Christina Maslach that I got it. No wonder I was so exhausted. I had sold my soul, my body, my life, and my well-being to the corporation.

When I lost my job, I had a choice: I could go back to another corporate job and start my climb again or, I could do something different. This took some soul-searching and question-asking. You probably won't be shocked to hear that I *did* go to another corporate job. I knew the minute I walked in the door, however, that I had made a mistake. There was a knot in my stomach the entire three months I worked there. I let male co-workers beat me up with their words and tear me down until I no longer recognized myself.

When I was fired from that job I sank lower than I had gone before. I was a mess.

I managed to make it a quarter-century before my adrenals nearly failed, but a significant number of high-fliers (over-achievers) burn out within the first ten years of their career. [8]

You might read the following story from England of how bad burnout can get and think it's ridiculous. Who would sacrifice their health for a job? But for me and many others, our unworthiness drove us to this point.

"When the police pulled up behind a young, high-flying leader staring vacantly out of his car window on the hard shoulder of the M1, they tried to question him. He didn't know his name, where he was going or how he had arrived there. He was mumbling, "Must get the figures ready. Manager's on my back. Need to perform better to get promoted". He had just completed 15 continuous months of 14 to 16 hours a day with rarely a day off.

Back at his place of work, his manager, when

[8] The Guardian January 6, 2015 Howard Awbery

questioned by the police explained: "Corporate sends them to me to either make 'em or break 'em. Obviously, he wasn't made of the right stuff, so I broke him!"[9]

If you suspect you might be burning out, here are some common symptoms. How many of these do you have?

- Inability to function
- Overwhelming exhaustion
- Frustration
- Cynicism
- Sense of ineffectiveness and/or failure
- Waning productivity
- Low creativity
- Diminished interest in work and/or life
- Poor relationships
- Failing health: depression, aches and pains, more frequent colds, disease
- Inability to focus and/or concentrate
- Feelings that life is empty and meaningless

If several of the above symptoms speak to you, then you are probably in burn-out mode—or headed

---

[9] https://www.theguardian.com/women-in-leadership/2015/jan/06/how-to-prevent-corporate-burnout

there. And it's because you are stuck in the unworthiness cycle. Please read on.

By the time I lost my job I could check off every single one of these symptoms. I always felt like I was behind and failing in all areas of my life—especially at home. And all I wanted to do was sleep. I vividly remember my first few weeks of unemployment. I rolled out of bed, put on yesterday's clothes, took my son to school, came home, and went back to bed. I often walked around in my jammies and bathrobe most of the day in a self-induced fog. Around 2 p.m. I would think, "Holy crap, it's almost time to pick up my son from school. I guess I better shower and dress." I tried to hide from my family how depressed I was and how I had wasted my day.

What I needed at that time was deep rest, space to contemplate, and time to mourn the loss of my job, and my old life as I knew it. I wish I had known that being laid off was a blessing and an opportunity to heal my body, mind, and soul, and to create a life I wanted, instead of creating a life according to other people's opinions of what it should be. I now know I listened to other people because I felt too unworthy to make my own decisions.

My focus was not on the possibilities that were

available to me. My focus was on the pity party I was having for myself, a potent mix of self-loathing, disappointment, and beating myself up for being so blind. It did not take long for me to sink into an all-time low and a desire to isolate from the world. I was a failure and I did not want anyone to know it.

The one good thing about hitting bottom? Up was the only direction I could go. I started my long journey from unworthiness to worthiness.

I quickly saw how society is geared toward telling me I was "not enough" unless I did things like:

- Buy the product that would make me ageless
- Buy the exercise gadget that was guaranteed to create six-pack abs
- Take extravagant vacations to exotic locales.

You get the picture.

Striving to feel "I am enough" has created a society of people that are living rote lives, on autopilot, often in burnout mode. They drive to work unsure of the route they took, unaware if they stopped for all the stop lights, not really focusing on their driving because they have just gotten up to live another day in their quiet life of desperation feeling unworthy of anything different. These are the people that could be teaching your children or staffing emergency rooms, all making decisions based on the worthiness they are looking for outside themselves.

And what I realize now is how many people are right where I was—stuck in the unworthiness cycle year after year—and yet they have no idea they are there.

An Epidemic Unchecked

What happens when there is an epidemic and no one does anything? The world becomes chaotic. Everything feels out of control. Tragedies unfold like dominoes, one right after the other. We operate out of fear. Insomnia and depression are rampant. Our communication becomes volatile and unkind. People feel hopeless and start isolating until we become a disconnected society and stop helping each other. Does any of this sound familiar? Seem a little like our world today? If we don't do something now, our deep unworthiness could lead us to catastrophe.

SUMMARY

Choosing to stay in the unworthiness cycle comes with a high price tag to your health and happiness. And yet it's insidious and hard to recognize when you're in the midst of it. Bombarded daily with news, advertising, and social media messages reminding you that you are not enough, you stay in the cycle that takes the joy, fun, and peace right out of your life.

The number one most dangerous symptom of unworthiness is one that is almost acceptable in our society. Burnout seems like an individual issue, but it's chronic, widespread, and costing corporations $150 to $300 billion dollars a year in lost productivity.[10]

When you move into the worthiness cycle, you choose to live in joy, have more fun, feel inner peace, be healthy, happy, and thrive. You are also giving society a fighting chance to thrive.

---

[10] https://workplacepsychology.net/2011/01/09/the-true-financial-cost-of-job-stress/

WORTHINESS

Chapter Five: What is Worthiness?

I've just spent the first section of the book talking about the Unworthiness Epidemic and why feeling unworthy is so rampant in our world. Now, I get to talk about something way more positive.

Worthiness.

Ahhhh.

Worthiness is your natural-born state. It is like the vibrant flowers on a colorful Hawaiian shirt. Bright. Colorful. Bold. When you leave the unworthiness cycle to walk in the worthiness cycle, you feel like you are invincible, like anything is possible. Think of how you felt skipping, zooming down slides, and swinging high on the playground swing. That's the same euphoric feeling that worthiness brings to your soul as an adult. Denying it is a choice, whether it is conscious or subconscious.

When you feel worthy, you dream big and take actions to make your dreams come true. You have self-confidence, self-worth, and self-love. Instead of comparing yourself to others, you celebrate the differences. You are excited for others' successes and encourage their dreams. Your approval, acceptance, and love come from within and can always be found there. You love to make decisions and know that all decisions can be modified and doing so does not require shame, guilt, or fear. There is a deep knowing that all is well and things are working in the right and perfect order. That all experiences in life are leading to where you want to go. Even the ones that may cause discomfort.

You wake each morning grateful for another day to live life to the fullest. You can't wait to get up and live your magnificent life. You might not need an alarm clock because you wake at the same time most days ready to greet the day with open arms. No need for that intravenous coffee, either. Your morning routine feeds and energizes your soul.

You have copious amounts of energy because you are being your authentic self— you're no longer pretending to be who you think others want you to be. At the end of the day you still have energy to do the things you want to do. When you go to bed, you think about all the things you finished and the empowering things you said. You feel magnificent, close your eyes with a deep sense of gratitude, and an excitement for tomorrow. You build yourself up with positive, life-affirming self-talk, and daily celebrations. You repeat this process day in and day out remembering how much you love your life.

Think this sounds impossible?

I wake up automatically at 4 a.m., write for three hours, meditate and journal, walk in nature, and then hop in the shower. But it was not until I reignited my own worthiness that I started waking up so early, exuberant to start my day. I do not want to miss a minute. Before my feet touch the floor, I list my gratitude. Thank you bed, for providing me with a comfortable night's sleep. Thank you blankets, for keeping me warm and dry. Thank you God, for gifting me with another day to go out and live life to the fullest. I get so stoked doing this, that I hop out of bed and into my bathrobe both arms at once and swiftly walk to my desk to start my daily writing. It is easy to become absorbed in the task at hand because it feeds my soul and is one of my passions.

Am I Worthy?

There are different levels of worthiness, just like there are different levels of unworthiness and you can go back and forth. I've created a test so you can see where you land.

I am sure you possess worthiness traits you can use

as building blocks. As you read through these symptoms, cycles, and behaviors, think about where they might show up in your own life. You may be surprised to learn that you already have some worthiness showing up in your life, and just not acknowledging it.

When you are worthy, you:

- Play BIG
- Have self-belief, self-confidence, and self-love
- Feel energetic
- Celebrate your successes
- Feel and act positive
- Break large tasks into smaller, easily managed tasks
- Feel hopeful and happy
- See an abundance of possibilities
- Are flexible
- Are authentic
- Expect good things to happen
- Honor your strengths, gifts, and talents
- Are fearless
- Sleep easily and well
- Embrace change and challenges
- Easily make decisions
- Build up other people

- Celebrate the successes of others
- Speak kindly to yourself and to others
- Have a great sense of purpose
- Feel a deep sense of connection with yourself and others
- Play the "What if..." Game instead of the "When I..." Game

Take the Worthiness Test

Ask yourself these questions to help you see the worthiness within you. Check the box for YES, NO, or SOMETIMES.

	YES	NO	SOMETIMES
Do you look at the events happening in our world and still feel hopeful?			
Do you want to make a difference and know that no matter how big or little your contribution, you are making a positive impact?			
Do you purchase retail goods because you like them and find them useful and you don't feel guilty about them?			

	YES	NO	SOMETIMES
Do you say, "Thank you" when someone gives you a compliment? (Compliments are gifts. Do you receive the gifts?)			
Are you comfortable enough to look into the mirror, right into your own eyes, and say, "I love you"?			
Are you living a life you love and enjoy?			
Does your life have meaning and purpose?			
Do you have days you feel alive, joyful, and excited about life?			
Does your work fill your soul?			
On the days you've been handed lemons do you still feel happy?			
Do you feel authentic when presenting yourself and your life to the world?			
Do you take care of yourself with a healthy lifestyle?			

	YES	NO	SOMETIMES
Are you happily married most days?			
Do you make decisions with ease and grace?			
Do you know that all decisions can be modified?			

If you answered "YES" to one or more of these questions, you are not starting from ground zero. You have experienced the worthiness within you. Perhaps you thought it was a fluke and only acknowledge it occasionally, but it is there and I promise you know how the worthiness cycle works. Now let's learn how to make it your norm and not just someplace you visit once in a while.

The Worthiness Workout

You were born with an unlimited supply of worthiness. You were taught unworthiness. If you have read this far, you know this.

And now you are faced with a choice. Do I stay in the unworthiness cycle—my uncomfortable comfort zone, where I know what will happen each time I take a spin in the cycle? OR do I step into the worthiness cycle and create a new comfort zone in the unknown?

Once you've decided, to stay in the worthiness cycle takes conscious daily action. It is not one of those things you can do for thirty days and poof, you're worthy. It takes daily care and feeding to maintain.

Think about how society constantly feeds your mind with messages of unworthiness and not being enough. That is coming at you 24-7, so you get to counteract society's negative messaging, you get to do it daily, and consciously.

I call it my Worthiness Workout and I look at going to my worthiness gym as a regular activity.

Here's what my daily worthiness workout looks like. (Find details on these and lots more in the TOOLS section.)

- List gratitude upon waking and throughout the day.
- Say my affirmations out loud in the mirror each morning.
- Look myself in the eyes in the mirror and

say, "I love you!"
- Meditate and journal.
- Take a gratitude walk in nature.
- TURNAROUND negative self-talk immediately.
- Eat organic, take supplements, and exercise to keep my worthy vibe high.

You can make the choice at any moment to see, acknowledge, and honor your worthiness. Because even though things may have gotten pretty bleak, your worthiness did not go away. It's like a pilot light inside you still lit, just waiting for you to see it, fuel it, and let it glow bright just like it did when you were born. Walking away from all you learned regarding unworthiness and walking in your magnificence and worthiness is scary. And it is the greatest gift you can give to yourself and the world.

When you are worthy you raise the vibration of the world and empower others to do the same. You go from discouraging to encouraging. Just by taking the first step for yourself, you empower others to do the same. It has a ripple effect across society.

So, I've been talking a lot about what can happen for you when you acknowledge your worthiness. Here's what happened for me.

As I ignited my worth, I saw the world around me change and it was because I changed. My relationships with my husband and my son improved. My health improved as I allowed myself the care I had so long denied. I felt more connected to people and worthy of the relationship instead of that lifelong feeling of being a square peg trying to fit into a round hole. Changing the way I viewed life changed *everything* in my world.

I could see that there was more than one way to achieve a dream; I could see more possibilities. Take my dream of being a CEO. I always thought I had to climb the corporate ladder to make that one a reality. I never, ever thought about being an entrepreneur, starting my own company and automatically being CEO. Yet, that's what I did. If I was still stuck in my unworthiness cycle I never would have seen that possibility.

Remember when I said that even when you are stuck in the cycle of unworthiness, you have moments of worthiness that appear from time to time. One place I had worthiness during my unworthiness years was when asking for salary. Money was a great motivation to climb the next rung of the ladder, even when it was hard. Then, when I would get the bigger salary, my unworthiness thoughts would kick in: Oh,

I need to work harder to prove I am really worthy of this big salary! What a vicious cycle, holding out hope that someday I would feel worthy enough to earn the number I had already achieved.

About three months after being laid off I started contacting recruiters to help me with my job search. I met with one and gave him my salary requirement, just slightly higher than my previous job. He told me that I would never get that much and that my salary requirement was $60,000 higher than the going rate in the industry. In that moment, I believed in my salary worth and knew that this recruiter was not the one to help me with my job search. I knew the rate he stated was what he *believed* to be true, but that was not my experience and I found article after article stating that the going rate for my position was much higher.

Two weeks later I landed a job for even more than my desired salary. I couldn't work with that recruiter because he did not believe in my salary worth and I'm not sure he believed in his own. His unworthiness lost him a lot of money.

SUMMARY

The worthiness cycle may be uncomfortable at first,

but it can quickly become a comfortable comfort zone. By moving away from learned negativity and unworthiness taught to you during your childhood, you are choosing to return to your natural born state of worthiness. Take the Worthiness Test so you can see you are not starting from ground zero.

By creating your own Worthiness Workout, you are committing to daily conscious action to combat and discern the negative bombardment of unworthiness messages that are thrown at you daily—you are choosing the worthiness cycle. You see the boundless opportunities available. You are empowering, encouraging, and your vision of the world changes. Choosing worthiness is a gift you give to yourself and the world.

As you become more comfortable in the worthiness cycle, you will not want to go back to the unworthiness cycle ever again. And if you do decide to visit, you will quickly leave remembering the uncomfortable comfort zone it presented.

Chapter Six: The Worthiness Cycle

Stepping into the Worthiness Cycle requires a conscious decision. It's scary at first because you are stepping into the unknown or at least a way of being you're not yet comfortable with. What's amazing about the worthiness cycle is you get to make choices that create different results. Plus, you get to know that all decisions you make are not permanent. They can be modified or tweaked in order to keep you in the worthiness cycle. In this chapter, we'll look at how the worthiness cycle operates—and how to make it your norm.

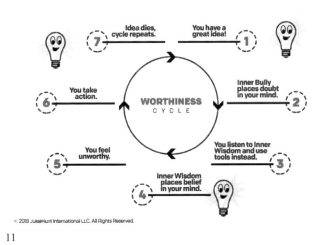

11

---

11 Graphic by Jenna Balogh www.jennabalogh.com

Like the unworthiness cycle, the worthiness cycle always starts with a great idea—a light bulb moment that you're excited about. Let's use the same example we used previously: You decide to start an exercise program. This is a great idea because it makes you feel better, gives you more energy, and improves your health. You have decided to go to the gym five days a week before work.

Day One: You set your alarm earlier than normal so you can hit the gym nice and early. The night before, you packed everything you need for your workout and for work so you can go directly to the office from the gym. The alarm goes off and because you are excited about your great idea, you hop out of bed, grab your bag and off you go to the gym. Afterward you feel proud of yourself for implementing the new idea. You have stepped into the worthiness cycle!

Day Two: The alarm goes off early again. You get up with a little less enthusiasm, but you made a commitment so you grab your bag and off to the gym you go. Afterward you feel energetic and happy. You are so glad you got up even though you were tired when the alarm went off. You vow to go to bed earlier to avoid that feeling tomorrow.

Day Three: The alarm goes off early. You are ready

to go because you went to bed earlier the night before. You remembered your vow and felt a lot more rested when the alarm went off. In the car on the way to work you are smiling because this time it feels different. Your decision still feels good, you feel different, and it is only the third morning.

Day Four: The alarm goes off early. This time you hit the snooze button once. You get up ten minutes later, then realize you did not pack your bag the night before so now you are even later than expected. Your Inner Bully starts to chatter at you. But you have been here before and you know how this movie ends. You decide to listen to your Inner Wise Woman instead. She says, "It is OK to be imperfect. Do the best you can. You can even choose to modify your decision."

You begin feeding your mind positive affirmations. You remember how good you felt after your workout yesterday. You quickly pack a bag and make it to the gym for a shorter session. As you are getting dressed for work you realize you have on two different color shoes. You laugh at your mistake and head home to fix your shoe faux pas. Now you are late for work and stuck in traffic. This gives you a chance to listen to uplifting music and sing in the car. Your Inner Wise Woman reminds you this is still a great idea and maybe three days a week would be a more realistic goal. You decide to stick with the five days for a few weeks and then make a decision. You are choosing to stay in the worthiness cycle.

Day Five: The alarm goes off. You jump out of bed, grab your bag and head to the gym. You are feeling pretty good about your great idea despite that midweek mishap. You chose to silence your Inner Bully, listen to your Inner Wise Woman, and take action from that place.

The worthiness cycle feels SO different from the unworthiness cycle. You feel more optimistic, invincible, and full of hope. You take life less seriously. You have more energy. You have successfully convinced yourself that you are worthy of the many benefits the exercise program will bring you. And you start to feel like this was a good idea to bring to life.

Week Two: You celebrate because you made different choices and created new results. You feel worthy of your great idea and your ability to see it through another week. You are creating a new comfort zone. You say to yourself, "So this is what it feels like to see an idea through to fruition. Wow! This is exhilarating."

By the end of the week, you are in your new comfort zone, letting your Inner Wise Woman run the show and feeling like a badass, worthy of success.

***

You tried on a new way of being and while it may not have felt comfortable at first, eventually it feels like it fits well and gives you confidence to keep going. You feel curious and confident about trying out more new ideas and seeing them through to fruition. You realize that each new idea can be modified and that it is still a success.

The most successful people in the world have failed their way to huge success by staying in the worthiness cycle when they could have easily felt very unworthy.

- Oprah Winfrey was publicly fired from her first television job as an anchor in Baltimore. She went on to create the number one daytime show and a media empire that empowers people to be the best they can be.
- Despite Thomas Edison's teachers telling him he was "too stupid to learn anything," he went on to hold more than 1000 patents and invented world-changing devices like the phonograph,

electric lamp, and a movie camera.

- When Sidney Poitier first auditioned for the American Negro Theatre, he flubbed his lines and spoke in a heavy Caribbean accent. The director angrily told him to stop wasting his time and go get a job as a dishwasher. He eventually became a hugely successful Hollywood star and helped break down the color barrier in the American film industry.

- J.K. Rowling was a single mom living off welfare when she began writing the Harry Potter series and became the first billionaire author with those seven books.

- Dr. Seuss had his first book rejected by twenty-seven different publishers.

- Walt Disney was fired from the Kansas City Star because he lacked imagination and had no good ideas. Today his creations ignite imagination in people of all ages.

It does not matter what your background is, where you come from, or how many setbacks you have had. You get to choose whether those experiences determine your worthiness or your unworthiness. Because you have a failure when taking a chance on your great idea does not mean you have to return to the unworthiness cycle, where failure is just more proof that you shouldn't bother trying. When you live in the worthiness cycle and experience a fail, you know that you get to learn from it.

Know Your Triggers

How you react to common triggers determines which cycle you end up in. We all have the ones that "get" us. Maybe for you it's when someone says something critical about your idea or your progress. Me, it's my "shitty shoulds" that kept me in the unworthiness cycle. It was uncomfortable because I had decades of going to parties, staying in jobs, hanging out with certain friends because "I should"—and putting my own dreams and desires on the back burner. Your triggers show you where you can rely on your Inner Wise Woman to help you make different decisions and get new results.

My Inner Wise Woman speaks to me gently, nonchalantly reminding me that I have been here before and I have choices. She encourages me, lifts me up with her words, and helps me see options filled with possibility. The question I ask when I'm facing a decision (or pushing the snooze button or reaching for a piece of chocolate cake) is, "How do I want to feel?" If I want to feel crummy I turn left and enter the unworthiness cycle. If I want to feel happy and excited I turn right and enter the worthiness cycle.

I have learned how to change the dialogue in my head, one of the most crucial things to do to stay in the worthiness cycle. When my Inner Critic shows up I thank her for stopping by and I let her know that I hear her concerns. I then give her a new role of Observer and I make a conscious decision to listen to my Inner Wise Woman instead. My Inner Critic keeps me in the unworthiness cycle and stuck in fear. I know my Inner Wise Woman will keep me in the worthiness cycle and makes me feel invincible.

That time I finished the half-marathon in three hours, I let the dialogue win and my Inner Bully tossed that accomplishment to the curb. Had I let my Inner Wise Woman speak to me she would have seen the accomplishment and the learning associated with the event.

She might have said something like:

As I reflect on my first half marathon, I realized I learned a lot. First and foremost, I have the choice to dub this a success or failure. I choose success. I had several setbacks during my training and overcame them all. I learned that when I have a persistent pain it means something is wrong. I learned that I stepped up to the plate when others did not even try. I learned that I was able to commit to the goal, start it, train for it, and execute it. I learned it does not matter how long it took me, I finished it. I finished thirty-two out of fifty-six people in my age class. I wasn't first, I wasn't last. I finished and I have the medal to prove it. I learned I can do it and once my hernia is fixed I am sure my next half marathon will be better."

That's right, I ran another half marathon! My time? 2:30:49. And I felt worthy before and after crossing the finish line and would have felt that way no matter what my time!

SUMMARY

It takes some practice, but the worthiness cycle becomes a comfortable comfort zone because you're walking in your natural born state of worthiness. Instead of always listening to your Inner Bully, you can choose to listen to your Inner Wise Woman and her messages that uplift you and keep you in the worthiness cycle. You are taking conscious daily action to feed your mind with positive messages to counteract the negative ones you're bombarded with throughout the day. You know that being human does not require perfection and even while you are in the worthiness cycle you can fail or have false starts and know that these lead to greater successes. You are quick to recognize your triggers and remind yourself you have been here before and you get to make new decisions to get different results. The worthiness cycle becomes familiar because it is the place you were born to live!

Chapter Seven: Symptoms of Worthiness

There will come a time when the worthiness cycle feels like home. When you've made a conscious decision to live in the worthiness cycle—your natural born state of being—you will welcome with open arms all invitations to learn and grow. In this chapter, I share the ten most common symptoms of worthiness I've discovered, and the very clear moment I realized I was experiencing it.

You Play Big

In 2004, my husband, ten-year-old son, and I decided we would take a year off and travel the United States in an RV. We went from our 4,000-square-foot home to a 350-square-foot 5th wheel and along the way shed our house, our community, our income, and our stuff. We pulled out of Atlanta, Georgia, with no plan other than to adventure, enjoy, and see the many splendors our country has to offer.

This sounded scary to many of our friends and family. The thought of no routine, no income, no plan, no home base, and no structure was more than some people could handle—and they did not hesitate to tell us their fears and worries.

I, on the other hand, was most excited, could not wait to unload, clean out, declutter, and get rid of the stuff I had accumulated during my shopping-addiction phase of unworthiness. An overwhelming task, but I knew that if I took one cupboard at a time, I could get through it.

I was choosing to play big. I wanted this. And I had complete confidence that I could bring this bucket-list idea to fruition. Even on the days when doubts crept in, I chose to walk in faith and believe that I was worthy of this adventure and that everything I needed would be handed to me as I needed it. If I had chosen to take a turn in the unworthiness cycle, my Inner Bully would have very easily talked me out of it. Not this time. I listened to my Inner Wise Woman and let her be my guide. Playing big like this was a sure sign I was feeling worthy.

Playing big means different things to different people, but it's all about taking that next step toward what you really want. You might feel a tinge of fear as you step into a new role at work, for instance, but you know that believing in yourself, your abilities, and your worthiness will empower you. You have faith and a deep knowing that even though this position might be much bigger than your original vision, you got this. You know the Universe has your back and will see you through.

Your Positivity is Contagious

When I first had my lightbulb moment about taking the RV trip, I knew that I first had to get buy-in from my hesitant husband and son. I needed to market the idea to them before they could join me in the spirit of "YES, let's do it!"

One evening at dinner I broached the subject. I talked about how we had always discussed taking an extended RV trip, but for whatever reason, we never planned it. We had just learned that three of our friends had been diagnosed with cancer and one was told she would die within weeks. Life is short, I told them. Do we want this dream to go to the grave with us, unfulfilled? Isn't now the time to bring this decade-old idea into reality?

I described how we could homeschool our son, and visit many landmarks, national parks, and sites of interest as we wanted. I showed them the numbers I'd calculated to prove we could make it all happen on the proceeds of our home sale and still have money left to start anew in another city.

I was positive about the idea, confident we could make it happen and that it would be fun. Our son was a resounding "YES" and could not wait to tell his friends. And once I assured my husband we would have enough money, he said, "Yes, let's do it." Had I approached this idea with a negative mindset, it never would have made it to the dinner table for discussion.

When you are positive, the impossible becomes possible. You see options you might never have seen. And I'm no scientist, but you look a whole lot better, because being positive seems to turn back the hands of time. The day after everyone decided they were in, I felt like a twenty-year-old—with a big, beautiful idea that I was going to bring to fruition. Even though I had a huge task ahead of me, my positive attitude made it exhilarating. I had a new spring in my step, was smiling and laughing more, and was excited to get up and live life with this new adventure on the horizon.

When you choose the worthiness cycle, you present a positive attitude to the world. You see the glass as half full. You expect good things to happen and they do. You become a magnet for goodness. You know how to manifest what you want in life and do it with ease and grace.

Your Happiness Lasts

When my son graduated from college, I was grateful for his success, but I admit I struggled with my new role—no longer mother, more like friend. Before I could move into it, I had to grieve the loss of our prior relationship. I definitely had some lower energy days.

Was I unhappy? No, I was just working through all the emotions, something you know about if you're a mom. While I had raised him to be an independent, contributing, loving, and worthy member of society and I knew my own worth beyond being a mom, I was also going to miss what we had.

When you are living in the worthiness cycle, happiness is your natural state of being. But that doesn't mean you're upbeat, bubbly, and overly excited all the time. You find that you have way more upbeat days, though, and that sadness is fleeting. In the worthiness cycle, you reaffirm the fact that your happiness comes from within and external factors only enhance it; your happiness is not created by them.

You might be saying, "But when my boss gives me kudos for a job well done in a meeting, that makes me happy."

That's great—but is that lasting happiness or just a temporary good feeling? Lasting happiness is an emotion that comes from deep within you—regardless of what your boss does.

Your Validation Comes from Inside

I used to believe there was only one way to achieve my goal to be a CEO and that was by climbing the corporate ladder, rung by rung. The only problem with that is that every promotion had to come from someone else. All my worth was in the hands of my boss. It took getting laid off to see that there was a path to CEO that did *not* require someone else seeing my worth. As I began to see my own worth I saw that I could be an entrepreneur, start my own business, and be the CEO of my own company.

I made the decision to climb the corporate ladder to become a CEO, later modified my plan, and achieved my goal by following a different path.

With self-confidence you keep and maintain your own power to the point that the external world cannot affect it. You're the one in control of you—and anytime the external world tries to tell you differently, you look within and do a gut check to see if what they say resonates with you—just like I taught my son to do when he was little.

You'll discover your self-worth is deeply rooted within you, a pilot light glowing brightly. Your job or spouse don't make you worthy, they merely enhance your self-worth. I call them worthiness accoutrements. And if the job or spouse go away, your self-worth stays intact. You may feel disappointment or sadness, but your essential worthiness hasn't changed.

When you need to make a decision, you look within for answers—not to others. You may do some research to help gather information, but deep down you know the answers reside inside you and all you have to do is listen for the answer. When people want to help you and offer advice, you have an internal discernment that can easily take what they say into consideration or move their input out of the equation. By relying on your own worthiness, decisions become easy. You also know that all decisions can be modified and altered as needed.

You Play the "What if…" Game

When you are in the worthiness cycle, you stop playing the "When I…" Game. You can see the possibilities and know they are endless. Instead of waiting for the other shoe to drop, you ask questions like this:

What if…

- This works?
- This idea helps millions of people?
- By doing X, Y, Z it is easier?
- This idea helps our world thrive?

By playing the "What if…" game, you are drawing on your unlimited supply of worthiness to see the multitude of possibilities that exist with each new idea and you draw to you the people, information, and circumstances to make that idea come to fruition. You expect great things to happen and they do. You do not view failure as the end of the world, but as a doorway opening to a new and better way to do things. As an opportunity to grow and learn.

The "What if…" game is very different from the "When I…" game that puts conditions on your happiness. Asking "What if…" allows new possibilities. For those of you asking if you couldn't use "What If" in a negative manner, such as, "What if…this doesn't work?" Yes, you could, but a worthy person would ask questions in the positive and not the negative.

As I cleaned out our overstuffed house, I stored all the things we were releasing in the garage. Eventually we could no longer park the cars there. As our estate sale approached, the task of sorting, displaying, and pricing items became more and more daunting. I was not even sure how to begin. So I used "What If…" and asked, "What if this task is easier with the help of some friends?" I put out an SOS in the neighborhood and one day several friends came to do the sorting, displaying, and pricing. At the end of the day, we'd created a well-organized store with different departments. There was a tent full of holiday items, toys were sorted into bins, a kitchen section, furniture, and so forth.

You Empower, Uplift, and Take Responsibility

Whenever I am having a difficult day, I find that if I go out into the world and give away smiles and compliments, my difficulties disappear. One day I was a little low. I went to a coffee shop drive-thru and paid the barista for the car behind me. The woman was so grateful that she honked her horn and waved to me as I drove away. It made me feel good to have created a bright spot in someone else's day.

As you walk in your worthiness, you empower others with uplifting words of encouragement. You take responsibility for your own life and do not blame others for your happiness or unhappiness. You look for ways to encourage yourself and others to follow their dreams. When you do this, you lift yourself up at the same time. When you take responsibility for your own life you hold onto your power. You are consciously creating your life and not leaving it in the hands of others. You decide what is important to you and make your own decisions. The result? You live a life you love.

You See the Perfection in Everything

I can look back and see the perfection in my layoff now, though at the time it felt like a devastating failure. Had I been in the worthiness cycle I would have been able to walk in faith that my corporate career was just a stepping stone to something bigger.

My diagnosis of adrenal fatigue is another perfect moment, because it allowed me to stop, rest, rejuvenate, and heal my body before I got really ill. And I saw that it was time to find work that filled my soul and allowed me to be with my family more. The diagnosis saved me from sitting on my deathbed and wishing I had worked less. Instead, it gave me a chance to do life and work differently. How perfect is that?

I marveled as my son moved from infant to toddler and how each phase of learning new things led to the next. First, he rolled from his tummy to his back and vice versa. Then he learned how to rock back and forth on his hands and knees, which led to crawling and, eventually, walking. Of course, I could see the perfection in each phase. Your worthiness journey is similar in that each phase is leading to something new and more exciting.

Perfection exists even when it feels like it's not there. You get to look for it when you think it is not present. This is how life unfolds when you walk in the worthiness cycle. You know deep in your soul that none of life's experiences are wasted. Each one is leading you to the next best step—the one with the highest and best outcome. When you are in the worthiness cycle, you walk in faith that this is your truth every day.

You Set Clear Boundaries

I used to think my friends should drop everything to take a call from me—especially one of my crisis calls, which were frequent. After all, I'd drop everything for them, so I couldn't understand why they wouldn't do the same for me. Turns out I had no boundaries and I did not respect theirs. Now, before

I call a friend I will text asking if she has time for a call. If the answer is "Not right now," I know she's busy and the greatest gift I can give her is space and understanding.

When I first started meditating, I put it on my calendar as daily *self-care*. I was setting a boundary by scheduling it, which meant I could not schedule anything else at that time. This empowered me: I would see it on my calendar, and sit down to meditate. I always felt calmer, more centered, and focused afterwards.

Then gradually, I started scheduling over it or blowing by it—another "leaky boundary." I did not honor my own boundary. I didn't yet fully believe that I was worthy enough to give myself fifteen minutes of self-care per day.

Today, my meditation time is sacred. I have set a self-care boundary that neither I nor others can cross. It is a necessity, not an option.

You might think that others disregard your boundaries because they do not see your worthiness. In reality, you're letting them trample your boundaries because you're not in the worthiness cycle. When this happens, put some space between you and the other person and check in with yourself to see where you are not honoring your *own* boundaries. This brings you back into the worthiness cycle and allows you to address the issue with the other person. Sometimes she won't understand because she is stuck in her own unworthiness cycle and cannot comprehend why you would want to be so strict or why it is so important to you. I have had to let people in my life go because they consistently tested my boundaries, but I always take a look at myself first and what I'm allowing.

When you are in the worthiness cycle you set clear boundaries without drama. You easily recognize when boundaries have been crossed and when you need to set a boundary. By setting boundaries you are taking care of yourself. If you don't take care of yourself, eventually you have nothing left to give. Setting boundaries is one of the greatest gifts you can give to yourself and your family.

For instance, when we made the decision to take the RV trip, people reacted one of three ways:

- They were excited for us and congratulated us.
- They said, "I could never do that."
- They let us know they thought we were crazy and had lost our minds.

I set a boundary that I was going to surround myself with the first group, rather than the naysayers.

Setting boundaries is a key component of worthiness. You are giving yourself the space you need to be you, to examine your own feelings and determine if they are yours or someone else's feelings. Boundaries enable you to stay in the worthiness cycle!

You Live in Abundance

One month I thought we were going to be short one-hundred dollars and that I'd have to pull money from savings to cover the shortage. I was walking in my worthiness cycle, though, and knew that it would all work out. Out of the clear blue sky I was refunded one-hundred dollars from a doctor's office that had overcharged me without my realizing it.

Had I been in my unworthiness cycle, I would have let my Inner Bully take over and berate me about not being more careful with my spending and having to pull from my savings account. Instead I chose to be in the worthiness cycle and have faith that the money would appear one way or another. Whenever money comes in I feel abundant. When I am surrounded by friends I feel abundant. When I look at the experiences I have had in my life, I feel abundant. I can only see this when I am in the worthiness cycle. Abundance comes in many forms. Love, time, money, friends, or experiences. In the worthiness cycle you feel abundant in all areas of your life. You know that you will always have enough money to pay your bills, take care of your needs, help others in need, and have fun. It is never a doubt. And when you feel abundant you easily let go of unnecessary things and unhealthy relationships because you know they will not take your worthiness with them. You may feel sad, but your worthiness stays intact.

You spend money to keep the flow of money into your bank accounts flowing freely. You charge for your services what you are worth. When you can see the abundance in all areas of your life, it feels good, easy, and comfortable.

You're Open to Trying New Things

When I was feeling unworthy I did not want to try new things because I feared I would fail, look like a fool, and other people would think I was unworthy. The only person, of course, who thought those things was me.

Selling our home and worldly goods to go on an RV adventure for a year was definitely trying a new thing. It required me to keep seeing with the eyes of possibility. Ultimately, I didn't care what others thought about our decision. I knew it was right for us and that was all that mattered.

It's a little arrogant to think other people sit around thinking about your life and what you're doing. Maybe there are some gossips in the world who do nothing but that, but they are never tending to their own life when they are tending to yours. Why is that? Because they are most likely living in the unworthiness cycle and looking for someone else's failures to make them feel better.

Trying new things, going on adventures, and being willing to learn and grow means you are in the worthiness cycle. You look and feel younger, your mind stays sharper, you are enjoying life more, experiencing more joy, and laughing a lot. Wouldn't you rather feel this way than live a miserable, rote life that ages you more quickly, is boring, and lacks joy, fun, and laughter? I hope you say yes to living in your worthiness cycle and choosing a grand life.

SUMMARY

The symptoms of worthiness are many. You do not

need to possess all of them to feel worthy. The world's MO is to throw as many messages of *doubt* and *not being enough* at you to trigger your unworthiness. That is why it's crucial for you to consciously tend to your worthiness daily. Use the Tools section to create daily routines and rituals that help you do this. I meditate, journal, and read affirmations daily. It is part of my Worthiness Workout.

You get to choose to empower yourself and others to walk in the cycle of worthiness. When you make this decision, you are saying "YES" to yourself and the world benefits from that decision.

Chapter Eight: The Rewards of Worthiness

When you choose to stay in the worthiness cycle, you heal past and future generation's genetic code from unworthiness to worthiness. This means worthiness becomes the norm in future generations.

Here's what a worthy society looks like:

People are healthy and rarely visit the doctor. They are vibrant and thank their healthy cells each morning because they're filled with gratitude for how fantastic they feel. They take responsibility for their life and decisions. When things go awry, they look for the learning and see the possibilities that arise. They know how to discern incoming information and protect their worthiness by watching and reading news, social media, and movies that focus on positive stories. A society of people who have control over their own destiny are destined to thrive for generations to come.

A worthy society is not fazed by the "I'm not enough" messages advertising sends, and eventually advertising becomes positive and uplifting. Credit card debt is minimal and millions of people pay off their credit cards each month. They live within their budget and use the credit card to earn miles or points, not because they don't have the money to pay for purchases.

After I finished my post-layoff pity party, I decided to work on me. I began reading books, attending workshops that empowered me and gave myself tools to change my thinking, and started believing in me. Using the tools every day, I gained the power to step away from the unworthiness cycle and into the worthiness cycle. I saw changes happening in my life. My glass was suddenly half full. Good things began happening on a regular basis and I felt worthy of all of them. I stopped waiting for the other shoe to drop and started expecting good things to happen. Changing my thoughts from negative to positive took the blinders off my eyes so I could see all the possibilities available to me. Life became easier and fun. Lines started disappearing from my face as years of stress and doubt fell away. I was authentically me and no longer pretending to be what society dictated. I moved away from the "shitty shoulds" and into the possibilities that could happen.

Relationships with my family greatly improved. I let people go who did not support me. This opened the door for new people to enter—people who did support me and lift me up. I created balance in my life and moved away from burnout. The new spring in my step made me feel like I was walking on air. I had a smile on my face that made my eyes sparkle. Weight dropped off my body because I was no longer stress eating. I wanted to take care of my mental and physical health and scheduled daily self-care to make sure it happened.

I let go of striving to be perfect, and chose to see all of life as perfection as is. I was able to see perfection in the supposedly "bad" things like losing my job. That was a gift that led me to writing this book and allowed me to see my real purpose for being on this earth. I started dreaming again. I consciously used my thoughts, words, and actions to create a life filled with joy, fun, laughter, and meaningful purpose. A life that filled my soul.

Our RV trip ended up being a beautiful training ground of worthiness. We were headed to Arizona to visit my mother-in-law for Thanksgiving when we saw the sign for Chiricahua National Monument and decided to check it out. I immediately wanted to stay and called my mother-in-law to let her know we were going to be a couple more days.

The next day we went hiking and when we got to the top of the park and looked out over the wonderland of rocks, it was unbelievable. The rocks created pillars in a multitude of shapes and sizes, some so top heavy they seemed to defy gravity. The sunset changed the colors and personality of the scene every few minutes. I was speechless in the face of what my eyes were drinking in. I remember feeling exuberant and at peace and stood there just holding my husband's hand.

This impulsive stop had a profound impact on how I saw the world and how much beauty I had allowed myself to see. After that, I felt like I'd expanded my lens and was able to see more beauty everywhere.

In Pennsylvania, we stayed in a mountaintop RV park that looked out over a valley and a mountain range. It was gorgeous and we experienced the most rich and vibrant sunset while there. I just sat on the picnic table and let my eyes feast on the view God had put on my plate. It made me think about the life we left and how I would have been too busy to see or appreciate this beauty. I wondered what I had missed all those years. I was grateful for that moment and vowed to pay more attention to these types of events on a daily basis.

It was September 11, 2004 and several little towns in the valley below were recognizing and honoring the tragedy that had happened three years prior. We watched firework displays from above. It was a sight to behold. I was reminded of how our country had come together to heal the wounds of this tragedy and that we had witnessed history that will not be forgotten.

The next morning, our campground was enveloped in thick fog. We watched the sun come up and slowly clear the fog away. This was only a couple weeks into our trip and I knew we had made a good decision. My soul was filling with the beauty of nature and I felt so much freedom. Before we left, my soul had been screaming, "Let me out, let me out" and here I was doing just that.

Had I not made a conscious choice to step into the worthiness cycle, I would never have experienced the thousands of joys that came from our adventure. If I had stayed in the unworthiness cycle I would have let my Inner Bully talk me out of the trip. But because I was in the worthiness cycle, I was able to see the world through the eyes of awe and curiosity much like a child sees the world as they move from baby to childhood. Living in the worthiness cycle has given me gifts beyond measure.

SUMMARY

The rewards of the worthiness cycle far outweigh the high costs of the unworthiness cycle. Life is easier. When you get a lemon thrown your way, you make lemonade. You have more fun, laugh often, and have more energy, not to mention that you age more slowly. You stop believing the myths society and media try to plant in your head. You start believing in possibilities. You stop judging yourself and others and start seeing the magnificence each person possesses. You often see it in others before they see it in themselves and you encourage and empower them to walk in their own magnificence. By doing this, you are helping our world heal and thrive. What a gift to the world.

TOOLS

Tools to Ignite and Maintain Your Worthiness

It's critical that you use your own tools to fill your mind with worthiness messages so you can combat the constant messages of unworthiness society and your Inner Bully throw at you. In this section, I share all the tools I used to reignite my own worthiness and stop listening to the bullshit the outside world offers so freely. These tools continue to empower me daily and strengthen my own discernment. I previously touched on a few of these; use this section as a reference guide to all the tools.

Whenever I get off track I refer to the tools and make sure I am feeding my worthiness daily. I consistently pull from my bag of tools to keep my worthiness intact and ignited. I take the maintenance of my worthiness seriously and I tend it consciously and on purpose. This is what has enabled me to create a life I can't wait to jump out of bed and live!

I've broken the tools down into four categories.

- Worthiness Workout Tools
- Self-Love Tools
- Self-Talk Tools
- Super Boosters

Where is the best place to start after an entire lifetime of being told you are not enough? Start with your thoughts and self-talk. After all, they create your life. They are instructions that you are sending out to the Universe the same way you give an order to a waitress in a restaurant. Begin by ordering what you want and *not* what you don't want. And whatever you do, be kind to yourself.

You are in learning (or, more accurately, *un*learning) mode. You are unlearning unworthiness and reigniting the worthiness you were born with. Be kind to yourself as you begin to work with the tools.

DAILY WORTHINESS
WORKOUT TOOLS

These are the Worthiness Workout tools I use daily. Like going to the gym, you can choose to use specific tools a few times a week or every day. I prefer to let no more than a day go by without using them. When I go longer, I feel myself slipping back into old habits or thought processes that do not serve me.

Monitor Your Self-talk

Consciously listen to what you say to yourself. The mind is a powerful thing. Remember that simply by changing your thoughts you can improve or eliminate the chemical imbalance in your body— without prescription drugs!

I started with a little notebook I carried with me at all times. Each time I had a negative or unworthy thought, I would stop and write it down. In the evening, I pulled out the notebook and took each negative thought and used the TURNAROUND (in SELF-TALK TOOLS) to turn each negative into a positive.

I admit the first few nights I looked at the notebook, I found myself wanting to berate myself for all the negativity I fed my mind. I had no idea how thoroughly I tended my negativity garden. So, I began using the best fertilizers and started tending my worthiness garden daily.

At the top of my page I wrote in big bold letters –

THIS IS A STARTING POINT!
I AM RE-IGNITING MY WORTHINESS!
STAY POSITIVE!
I AM TENDING MY WORTHINESS GARDEN!
I WAS BORN WORTHY!

This was my reminder that beating myself up for not being kind to myself was *not* serving me. I was making a different choice about my life going forward and my efforts were going to create new outcomes. I was choosing to stay in the worthiness cycle.

Use Affirmations and Mantras

In her book, *You Can Heal Your Life*, Louise Hay taught me the power of affirmations. An affirmation opens the door and is the beginning point on the path to change. Consciously choose positive affirmations to eliminate an old negative pattern or create something new in your life.

It is important to remember to say them often and with

conviction, especially if you don't believe them. Remember, you are retraining your brain to ignite your worthiness. If "I am." feels too uncomfortable, start with, "I am willing to…" Then move into "I am…" I change my affirmations every month. I write them down during the new moon in my journal and tag that page. Each morning I stand in front of the mirror and read my affirmations. The more I say them, the more I believe them. Here are some examples:

- I am open and willing to love myself and receive love from others.
- I am kind to myself and to others.
- I love my family and my family loves me.
- I am healthy, wealthy, and wise.
- The world is a friendly place.

Mantras are medicine for the soul. It can be a word or series of words that you repeat over and over as you meditate. Mantras allow the meaning to settle into your subconscious helping you shift negative habits and patterns into positive ones. Here are some of my favorite ones.

- Release, Release, Release
- The Universe has my back
- Ram (means "our soul, super consciousness, truth and virtue")

- So Hum (means "I am that")
- Om (considered to have high spiritual and creative power)
- Love, Love, Love
- Make different choices; get different results
- All is well

Whenever I find myself stuck in an old story which keeps me in the unworthiness cycle, this affirmation quickly shifts me into the worthiness cycle. You are welcome to borrow my affirmation for yourself.

"I trust that everything is unfolding as it should. I trust the highest and best outcome for everyone is at work here. I believe in myself, my heart, and my worthiness. All is well. I am safe."

Have an Attitude of Gratitude

Nothing takes the wind out of unworthiness faster than gratitude. It is impossible to be grateful and negative at the same time. Gratitude raises your level of positivity and happiness. You can perform significantly better. Your intelligence, creativity, and energy all increase when you practice gratitude. And your brain scans the world for the positive—so important since we live in a negatively charged world.

Lori's Story

Lori Portka (www.LoriPortka.com) makes art with the intention to radiate love and healing. Several years ago, she decided to create one-hundred paintings for one-hundred people she was grateful for. She knew that the project would feel good, but did not expect the impact it would have on her marriage. Now, Lori and her husband try to notice what the other person is doing and thank them for that—something they did not do much of before the project. Lori says gratitude just grows and grows and the more she focuses on gratitude the more she is grateful for. Gratitude has made her world a lot bigger than it was.

Incorporate Gratitude into Your Worthy Life

- Start first thing in the morning. When you wake up, roll over and hug your bed and say thank you for such a comfortable sleep. Hug your pillow and say thank you for supporting my head and neck. Hug your blankets and thank them for keeping you warm and dry. Thank God for another day to live life fully and teach others to do the same. You will be so charged up and energetic that you will jump out of bed and into your pants both legs at once. It is a beautiful way to start the day.

- Take a gratitude walk during which you list all the things you have to be grateful for along the way.
- Start a gratitude journal and write in it daily.
- Make gratitude the first topic of conversation with your children at the dinner table or at bedtime tuck-in.
- List your gratitude at any moment and change your day from lousy to outstanding.

The next time you feel stressed, write down five things you are grateful for and see what a difference it makes in your state of mind.

Practice Meditation

Meditation is a big part of my daily self-care and my Worthiness Workout—and it keeps my worthiness flame glowing brightly. Starting a meditation practice can be daunting because there are so many forms. Try out a few to determine which one works for you. I use a variety of techniques depending on what I need at that time. Start slow and be kind to yourself. It is common for thoughts to run through your mind while meditating. Just let them come in and go out. Over time they will become fewer and fewer.

Here are different types of meditation:
- Walking meditation
- Journaling meditation
- Guided meditation
- Meditation with soothing music
- Silent meditation

Benefits of meditation:
- Relieves stress and anxiety
- Lowers blood pressure
- Brings answers to questions you have been asking
- Calms your mind
- Reduces over-activity in your body
- Brings you to center so you can produce and create easily
- Gives you a feeling of peace and contentment
- Decreases symptoms of depression
- Increases concentration and relaxation
- Overall improvement of general well-being

Keep a Journal

I have been keeping journals for years and it is fun to go back and see where I was and how much I have grown. Way back when, the blank page felt scary, so

I started with a gratitude journal in which I'd write three to five things I was grateful for each day. Remember, there is no right way to journal.

Here are some ideas and topics to inspire your journaling:

- **Spew journaling** is helpful when you're angry or upset about something. Write every angry thought you have on the paper. Sometimes I write so hard the pen rips the paper. I will write out the entire incident until it is all on paper. Then I burn it, releasing it into the ethers of the Universe. It always takes the edge off my anger.
- **Conversational journaling** is what I use to communicate with my Inner Wise Woman and get an answer to a question. I start with, "Dear Inner Wise Woman…", I ask my question and then write what comes into my mind. It is a powerful journaling exercise and has helped me gain clarity on many occasions.
- **Gratitude journaling** is the one I mentioned earlier. Simply write down the things you are grateful for. It can turn any negative into a positive because it's impossible to be negative and grateful at the same time.
- **Uplifting quotes**. I write these in my journal

to use in times when I need a reminder of how precious life is or to give me encouragement at a rough time.

- **Affirmations**. I create new affirmations each month at the new moon and write them in my journal so I can read them daily.
- **Happiness**. Write about something that enhanced your happiness that day—a beautiful flowering bush filled with new blooms, or a sunrise or sunset that filled your soul.
- **Sadness**. Write about something that made you sad that day—losing a pet or saying goodbye to a friend moving away.
- **Desires and Dreams**. Be bold and write them down. Let your heart sing and dream big.
- **Notes from self-improvement courses or workshops**. It's so easy to forget something that inspired you. What you write down increases the odds of actually implementing the learning.
- **Pictures or Photographs**. I sometimes draw pictures of things I saw that filled my soul or tape photographs in my journal that made my heart sing.

You can put anything you want in your journal. Make it yours.

Give Up Judgement

Giving up judgement was a tall order for me. It was ingrained deep inside my subconscious so I used the same tools as I used for my negative thoughts to work on judgement. I became conscious about when I was judging and would use the TURNAROUND to compliment someone instead of judging them.

When you stop judging yourself and others you see the magnificence in everyone. You become your own cheerleader and the one who cheers others on and encourages people to go one step further! The one who is quick to celebrate their accomplishments and good deeds. When you give up judgement you are choosing to be in the worthiness cycle and help others stay there, too.

Laugh Often

I once attended a laughter workshop. We each lay down on the floor with our head on someone's stomach. The first person in the chain started to laugh, which in turn made each person down the chain laugh. I still chuckle at that exercise and how fun it was. It totally took my mind off any unworthiness story I was telling myself. If you find yourself spiraling down into a negativity abyss, stop, and laugh for a few minutes.

Watch a funny comedy. Call a friend who always tells a hilarious story. It changes everything.

Adopt Rituals, Systems, and Processes

While taking my journey, I put some things in place to help me stay in the worthiness cycle and to simplify my life. I still do them. For instance, I have a quarterly ritual in which I write down all the things I accomplished and experienced for the last quarter: I include social events; memories created; progress on projects; changes in thoughts, words, or actions; A-HA moments and more. When you feel unworthy you forget to recognize your accomplishments along the way. By putting a ritual in place to do this on a regular basis you are choosing the worthiness cycle. Like all of us, I sometimes forget to acknowledge what I've done or accomplished, and I'm always amazed at how rich my life is when I do this ritual.

I also put some processes in place to keep me from beating myself up for tasks undone and stepping back into the unworthiness cycle. Expense Tracking was a huge one. When I was a corporate employee I turned in expense reports immediately upon return from a business trip. But as an entrepreneur, I'd put it off and put it off until it was the end of the year and time to get the paperwork together for my CPA. I would berate myself for waiting so long and then lock myself in my office for several days until it was done. It felt like punishment.

I put a process in place to stop this unpleasant cycle. I schedule an hour a month on my calendar to update my tax spreadsheets. As the end of the year approaches I have no reason to beat myself up because I chose to update my records monthly instead of waiting until the end of the year.

To help manage money I've created processes for weekly and monthly budgets and automatic withdrawals to my savings accounts. This way, money is available when large bills come in. And to insure I spend money wisely at the grocery store, I create a weekly menu and grocery list. This way I do not buy food that will go bad or that I do not need. Best of all, I never have to wonder what to make for dinner because it is on my weekly menu.

Daily, weekly, and monthly rituals and processes keep me in the worthiness cycle. I read my affirmations, list my gratitude, meditate, and journal daily. These are activities that I consciously use to bolster my worthiness.

Where do you typically let yourself down or beat

yourself up? Remove those opportunities by putting an easy process in place or creating a regular ritual.

Watch Uplifting Media

Instead of watching the news or getting drawn into a Netflix binge, watch an uplifting movie with a story of triumph or a positive message. I often listen to a Ted Talk or a Super Soul Sunday segment while I am getting ready in the morning. It is another way to start your day off in the worthiness cycle. Hop onto these sites:

www.youtube.com
www.ted.com/talks
www.oprah.com/supersoulsunday

Look up inspiration, motivation, or gratitude and check out one of the many videos that come up.

Look Within for Validation

Begin by asking yourself if you approve of yourself and your actions. When you do not approve of yourself, you have fallen back into the unworthiness cycle. Write your own personal review for yourself (think of it like a job review) in a positive manner and read it often.

Put your needs first and others' needs second. When you tend to your own needs first, you have more energy to share in helping others tend to their needs.

When making a purchase, check in with yourself and ask why are you buying this item? Is it because it will make you feel more worthy or because people will like or accept you more? Or is it because you think it will *add value to your life* or *you just want it because you like it*?

Here's an example: I used to buy clothing to fit in and so people would think I was fashionable. Now it seems silly making clothing decisions based on other people's opinions, but I did it all the time. The problem was that I bought things I did not necessarily like or feel comfortable in. Ugh! This meant I had a closet full of clothes like the mini skirt and platform shoes that I never wanted to wear.

Have you ever been standing in front of your overstuffed closet saying, "I don't have anything to wear"? That might be because you weren't buying those clothes for *you*. When I started buying clothes based purely on whether I liked a particular item and it was comfortable, my closet filled up with things I loved wearing each day. They were for my enjoyment and comfort, not the enjoyment and comfort of others. The bonus in this scenario is that because you love what you are wearing, other people tend to like it, too. Your "like" transfers to them and they can feel how great you feel in your own clothes.

Learn to Discern

Information Overload can lead to unworthiness. Staying in the worthiness cycle means being discerning when it comes to choosing how much information you take in. Is the message conveyed to you your own truth? How do you feel after spending time on social media? If you compare yourself to others on a social platform and come away feeling less than, it is time to discern the information you receive here.

You could:
- Spend less time on social media.
- Surround yourself with uplifting and supportive people on your social media sites.
- Congratulate and celebrate others because you are happy for them.

When you choose to walk away from negative, self-defeating messages, you are choosing to walk in the worthiness cycle.

Know Your *Own* Spiritual Beliefs

Use your common sense when it comes to choosing what and how you worship. Here's what I do: Take all the positive messaging and leave the negative messaging behind. I personally believe God is unconditional love and does not punish. (We do a very good job of punishing ourselves unnecessarily before we forgive ourselves.)

Understanding that all religion is ultimately about unconditional love is a belief that keeps me in the worthiness cycle—and that's where I want to stay. You don't have to believe what I believe. Take a look at what your religion believes and check in with each belief: Is it positive and does it keep you in the worthiness cycle?

SELF-LOVE TOOLS

Whenever you find yourself feeling low on self-love, pull one of these tools from your tool bag and get conscious and intentional about loving yourself.

Learn to Love Yourself Unconditionally

After spending decades hating myself, this was a tall order. I took Louise Hay's course, "Loving Yourself," in which she uses mirror work to teach you how to love yourself. At first, I could not look in the mirror and tell myself, "I love you." I kept at it until I could. This was empowering work that paid off and enabled me to make different decisions about my life and my self-talk. If you cannot look in the mirror and say, "I love you," try saying, "I am *willing* to love you." That way you are opening up the doors of possibility.

By eliminating old, conditioned thought processes that make you feel unlovable, you are choosing to stay in the worthiness cycle. Love yourself, no matter what. When you love yourself unconditionally you give others permission to do the same for you. One of my daily affirmations is, *"I am whole, perfect, and complete. I love me just as I am."*

You are a spiritual being having a human experience and humans are imperfect by nature. That is how you learn on your journey through life. Embrace and love every single part of yourself. You do not need to apologize for being worthy and loveable just as you are. Simply honor it.

Make Self-Care a Priority

Self-care is not a luxury. It's a love gesture to yourself. It is the greatest gift you can give yourself and your family. It is rejuvenating and feeds your soul. In our home, it is a necessity, not a desire. We schedule this sacred time on the calendar and do not schedule over it.

Imagine you have a pot of gold inside you and every time you do for others a piece of gold leaves the pot. What happens when the pot is empty? There is nothing left to give. If you keep giving from an empty pot of gold, you become resentful, angry, and tired. Self-care replenishes your pot of gold and keeps you in the worthiness cycle.

Ideas for self-care activities:

- Massages
- Yoga/Pilates
- Read an uplifting book. (Psycho thrillers don't work here.)

- Exercise. (If you hate exercise, this is not a self-care activity.)
- Walk or hike alone or with someone you enjoy (If you go with someone who pushes your buttons, it is not a self-care activity.)
- Gardening (Only if you love it. For me this would not be self-care, but sitting outside and enjoying *your* garden would lift me up!)
- A bubble bath with a "Do Not Disturb" sign on the door
- Music that makes your heart soar
- A dance session to a few of your favorite songs
- You decide what fills you up!

If you don't have a self-care list, now is the time to make one. Don't just make it and place it in the "someday" pile. Put it on your calendar. It won't take much time to fill your pot of gold, but you can't do it all at once. Add to it daily.

Trust Your Gut

When you hear something that does not sit right with you or feels like you might be heading back to the unworthiness cycle, check in with your gut. If what you hear does not match what your gut thinks, it is not your truth. You can then decide to let it go so you can stay in the worthiness cycle. Remember the story of my young son with his grandmother? Trust your gut. It is always right.

Send Love

When things don't seem to be going your way, feel difficult, or you find yourself dealing with a difficult person, love is the ultimate tool. Send love to yourself and to the difficult situation or person, and watch how the difficulty falls away. Love can dissipate any situation and is the most powerful emotion you can choose to use at any time. It frees you from the bondage of unworthiness and staying stuck in an old story. When you find yourself wanting to beat yourself up over not doing something perfectly, choose love instead.

The artist Anni Kemp (IntentionalGraffiti.com) taught me to use *Love* as my favorite four-letter word. She has an entire store of "Love Wear" and personal items to remind me to use love as a mantra. Whenever I want to wrap myself in *love* I wear one of her shirts or yoga pants. I feel love energy around me and this keeps me in the worthiness cycle.

Commit to Lifelong Learning

Every event that occurs in your life is an opportunity to learn and grow, even the experiences that don't feel so good. My divorce was an invitation to learn and grow. So was the loss of my job. I can look at both of these events and be grateful for them now.

Life is a classroom. The more you use it as such, the more you will stay in the worthiness cycle. For me, reading books; attending workshops, conferences, and retreats; and being part of a sisterhood that sees and accepts me, warts and all, are the ways I choose to keep learning continuously.

Pick books and movies that feed your mind food to keep you in the worthiness cycle. Take what resonates for you from each one and use it to fuel your worthiness.

Find like-minded people and spend time with them. Your conversations will fill your soul. Infinite Possibilities, Soulapalooza, Celebrate Your Life, Hay House, and spiritual retreats are some of the places I've met uplifting people who are also committed to learning and growing. The internet is filled with more possibilities than you can imagine. Pick one or two to attend each year. Go to local gatherings. Find free opportunities on www.meetup.com. Create a list of events to fill your mind and soul with the food that you need to stay in the worthiness cycle.

Celebrate Often

It's so crucial to acknowledge the steps you have taken and progress you are making on your journey from unworthiness to worthiness. This journey can seem daunting at first. When you stop and celebrate the successes, no matter how big or small, you are choosing the worthiness cycle. Let's say today you only had three negative thoughts and you used the TURNAROUND to turn them into positives. *That* is something to celebrate. Congratulate yourself and honor the steps you are taking. You can celebrate by doing a happy dance, scheduling some extra self-care, patting yourself on the back, or simply pausing to feel proud about your accomplishment. Just saying, "I acknowledge this success" can be a celebration.

Choose Your Friends Wisely

As I started my journey I realized that I had collected a lot of negative friends while in the unworthiness cycle. These were people I let tear me down, who always saw the glass half empty, and were unable to be responsible for their own lives, but knew what was best for everyone else's life. To be in the worthiness cycle I needed to surround myself with friends who would support me, lift me up, believe in me, and cheer me on. I had to let go of the friends who did not like my new attitude or who wanted to stay stuck in their own story. I did not make an announcement that we were breaking up—I just quit calling them.

What I realized was that most of my friendships when I was in the unworthiness cycle were one-sided; they only existed because I was initiating all contact between us. They never reciprocated. When I stopped calling I guess they did not miss me because they never called me either. By letting go of negative friends, you open the door for new positive friends to come in and enhance your life.

As for those negative family members you can't let go of, you can limit your contact with them. If you come away from your family gatherings feeling bad about yourself, reduce the time you spend with them and be positive while you're together. Or you can just smile and secretly send them love.

Be Authentic

We hear a lot lately about being authentic. Worthiness

is your original state of being. There's no need to pretend you are something other than your amazing self. Honoring your authenticity is being true to yourself and others. When you live authentically you are like a breath of fresh air because this is not how most of the world lives. It takes so much less energy to walk in your magnificence than it does to pretend to be what you think the world wants you to be. You are just being yourself—present, whole, and complete. Worthy of living fully and abundantly. Because there are no false pretenses here, people like to be around you. The cool thing is, when you stop presenting false pretenses to others, they do not feel the need to present them to you. What a relief!

Forgive and Forgive Again

Forgiveness is letting go of past events and the hope that they could have been different. It means you are no longer being held hostage by the past. It takes a lot of energy to hold a grudge. Forgiveness is something you do for yourself. You are letting yourself off the hook and ending the control lack of forgiveness has over your life. Forgiveness possesses a healing power. You are a spiritual being having human experiences—and humans make mistakes, missteps, and errors in judgement. Forgiveness is the tool you can use to keep you in the worthiness cycle.

When you do not forgive, you are choosing the unworthiness cycle.

Take Back What School Took

What parts of yourself did you start hiding from the world in an attempt to "fit in" during middle and high school? You may remember that I hid from my classmates that I competed in music competitions on the weekends and won. I did this because I did not think they would approve of me if they knew I was such a classical nerd. Think back to that time in your life and see where you denied magnificent YOU because you wanted to fit in or wanted outside approval. Time to dust those things off and honor them—even if it's just in your memory. Be proud of who you are and what you have accomplished. You were born magnificence in motion!

SELF-TALK TOOLS

If you find yourself slipping back into negative self-talk, these tools will help you silence your Inner Bully and empower your Inner Wise Woman.

The TURNAROUND

The TURNAROUND is simple. You take a negative thought and turn it into a positive one. The first conscious thing I did once I left my job was listen to my own self-talk. And, boy, did my Inner Bully control it! I did not use this realization to beat myself up more, however—I used it as a starting point to step into the worthiness cycle. Every time I heard a negative thought I would write it down. At the end of the day I used the TURNAROUND—turning those thoughts into positive ones. It took a little practice, but now I am probably the fastest TURNAROUND in the West.

Here are the typical negative thoughts I had—and their TURNAROUND.

- I am dumb became *I am smart enough—in fact I have two college degrees and a lifetime of wisdom in my brain.*
- I am unworthy of huge success became *I am worthy of huge success and all the goodness the world has to offer. In fact, the fruits of my success*

can be used to find cures for diseases and stop conflicts in our world.

- I am fat became *I am healthy and my body is the right and perfect size. Not to mention how sexy I am—I own it, baby!*
- I am ugly became *I am so pretty they had to increase the scale to eleven.*
- I am unlovable became *I am made of love. I love myself unconditionally and allow others to love me the same way.*

I wrote the TURNAROUNDs on three by five index cards and carried them with me. I put them in my lunchbox so when I opened my lunch I would be reminded to read them out loud. I had one on the dash of my car and read it at stop lights. I wrote on my bathroom mirror with a dry erase marker and read it morning and night. I was diligent about firing my Inner Bully and hiring my Inner Wise Woman, and sometimes had to do that over again every day. I was retraining my brain and I had lots of retraining to do because I had been tearing myself down for such a long time. By doing this I was gradually unlearning unworthiness and reigniting my worthiness. Little by little I peeled back the layers of unworthiness like you peel an onion. It did not take long to see the fruits of my labor impact my life in a positive way.

Stop. Cancel. Clear.

I learned this tool from Andy Dooley (andydooley.com) and it helped me implement the TURNAROUND more quickly. Each time I heard a negative thought, I said, "Stop. Cancel. Clear." This allowed me to stop the negative thought, cancel it out, and clear my mind for one of my TURNAROUNDs. I use this one frequently.

Shutdown your "Shoulds" and Change them to "Coulds"

I learned about the "Shitty Shoulds" from my own stellar coach Regena Garrepy (RegenaGarrepy.com). Listen to your self-talk. How many times do you start a sentence with, "I should…"? Write those down.

Here are some examples:

- I should live within my budget.
- I should eat healthy food.
- I should go to the gym daily.
- I should be kind to myself.
- I should save more money.

It is unkind to "should" all over yourself. "Shoulds" make you feel *less than,* resentful, and angry. They steal the joy out of your life and keep you in the unworthiness cycle. Try replacing "should" with "could." Should is riddled with shame and guilt. Could is filled with possibility. A simple word replacement changes meaning instantly.

Listen to the difference:

- I could live within my budget.
- I could eat healthy food.
- I could go to the gym daily.
- I could be kind to myself.
- I could save more money.

Tell a New Story

One day I was sitting in church when our minister, Reverend Carole O'Connell (caroleoconnell.com), asked the question, "Are you stuck in your story?" I listened carefully to what she had to say. She said that when you keep telling your story over and over, you are stuck in that spot and cannot move from it. You are reiterating that *this* is where you are supposed to be and shall evermore remain. Holding onto the past is what prevents you from accepting change. Clinging to the old and familiar doesn't stop change, it just keeps you stuck. She said that if you want to move past that story, you need to tell a new story. A story of where you want to be. The story you choose to tell will enhance your happiness and determine if you are in the worthiness cycle.

So, if you want to feel worthy, stop telling your unworthiness story. Stop talking about how your divorce ten years ago ruined your life or how you can't bounce back from a financial crisis. Tell a worthiness story until you believe it. When you tell your unworthiness story over and over you are sending instructions to the Universe that you want more life experiences like that to prove that you are supposed to feel unworthy. Send new instructions with a new story.

Change the Way You Look at Things

Dr. Wayne Dyer used to say, "When you change the way you look at things, the things you look at change." I have been married to my husband for nearly three decades and there are *still* days I question why I married him. Then I remind myself to change the way I look at him.

A few years into our marriage I would get so upset at all the things he did *not* do that I forgot to notice all the things he *did* do. When I decided to change the way I looked at him, our marriage got better. I decided to see all the things he did and say, "Thank you." As a result, he started doing more good things—or maybe I just noticed them more. Who knows? I chose to change the way I looked at him and it impacted our marriage in a positive way. He did not change; my view changed—from negative to positive.

SUPER BOOSTERS

Super Boosters are ultra-special, turbo-charged tools that will expedite your worthiness journey.

Visualize

Visualization takes very little time and creates amazing results quickly. Studies have shown that athletes who visualize more than they practice perform better in competition. Visualization is simply pretending and rehearsing in your mind—and keeps you focused on what you want. While shifting from unworthiness to worthiness, visualization will be one of your most important tools to spark fantastic life changes and it can be accomplished in just five minutes a day.

The mind does not know the difference between real and imaginary. Research has proven that with mental rehearsal, minds and bodies become trained to actually perform the skill imagined.

In their book, *Karate of Okinawa: Building Warrior Spirit,* authors Robert Scaglione and William Cummins describe a study regarding visualization among athletes. They studied four groups, ranging from those who did one-hundred percent physical training to those who did less physical and more visualization training. The group that performed the best was the group that did twenty-five percent physical training and seventy-five percent visualization training.

Guidelines for Visualization

These guideline were taught to me by Mike Dooley (tut.com), author of several books including *Infinite Possibilities—The Art of Living Your Dreams.*

- Practice visualization just five minutes per day – any longer than that and your mind will begin to wander. If you are a woman you will start thinking about your "to do" list and if you are a man you will start thinking about sex. You can visualize anywhere – in the shower, in bed before you go to sleep or before you get up, at your desk. Pick the time of day you want to visualize and make it a habit! Quality is far more important here than quantity.
- Imagine every possible detail of your worthy life — sights, sounds, colors, smells, activities, an ideal day, how you want to feel, etc. For example, if you want to run a marathon, imagine yourself crossing the finish line. What does it feel like to finish, to see your time, and to feel the cool breeze on your face? Who is there to greet you? Can you hear them cheering with excitement? Can

you smell the bananas waiting for you in the cool-down area as you walk off the lactic acid and celebrate what you just accomplished?

- Emotions energize and super charge your visualization and make things happen a whole lot faster. Feel the excitement, joy, pleasure, and victory. You might even say a little "yippy!" or "woop-de-do!"
- Put yourself in the mental pictures. Sometimes we visualize and forget to put ourselves in the picture.
- Be gentle with yourself. You are normal if negative thoughts pop into your head. Be patient with yourself – this takes practice. You may worry all day about losing your job and then come home and visualize for five minutes about your next promotion. Because of the intense passion and emotion associated with your five minutes, it wipes out your "all-day" worrying.
- Focus on one dream at a time. Visualize what your worthy life looks like and how it feels to be in the worthiness cycle.

Create a Vision Board

Another way to enhance your visualization is to create a Vision Board or Book and look at that while you are visualizing. I started with a Vision Book. I took a regular spiral notebook and put one of my visions on each two-page spread. I then found photos and words on the internet and in magazines to help me better imagine my vision. Creating a vision board helps you clarify your dreams and desires. It is a visual representation of everything you want to be, do, or have in your life.

Create a vision board that reminds you what your worthy life looks and feels like. Put it where you will see it daily. Visual cues like this help you stay in the worthiness cycle consistently. There are many resources on the internet on how to create a vision board.

Go on a News Diet

I love what Dr. Michael Bernard Beckwith says: "The only reason to watch the news is to create your prayer list." The news is designed to stir the emotional pot of the world. It catches people doing things wrong instead of right or it portrays them in a negative light. You could do ten amazing things in a day and then make a tiny *faux pas* and the news will report on your infraction. It was not always that way. There was a time when journalists reported the facts and did not over-sensationalize the negative aspects of the events that happened in our world. These days when you watch the news, your energy plummets and you can feel hopeless. It is easy to get stuck in the unworthiness cycle when you watch the news regularly. Try a news fast for ten days and see what impact it has on your worthiness.

Go Out and Play

Have you ever tried to remember someone's name and no matter how hard you try you cannot think of it? Then, when you are doing something different, out of the blue you remember their name? This is what *play* does for you. Play relaxes your mind so you can stay in the worthiness cycle. Schedule regular play into your day. This gives your mind a better chance of staying positive. Here are some ideas for play:

- Stop at a playground and swing or go down the slide
- Play a fun game with your children
- Join a baseball, basketball, or kickball league
- Build sand castles in the sandbox or at the beach
- Skip down the street
- Jump rope

What do you like to do for play?

Creative Time

Similar to play, creativity relaxes your mind so you can stay in the worthiness cycle. It allows your creative juices to flow so you can be more productive and creative. There are many outlets for creativity and it is good to try new creative outlets from time to time. Here are a few ideas.

- Creative writing
- Coloring (Get some cool adult coloring books and crayons)
- Scrapbooking
- Painting
- Knitting
- Sewing
- Woodworking
- Building projects
- Doodling

What creative activities do you like?

Turn off the Tech

Implement a low-tech day each week. Turn off your cell phone, PC, TV, and all other electronics. This removes comparison of others from your life and empowers you to stay in the worthiness cycle. It also gives your mind a break from the constant barrage of negative messages that tell you that you are "not enough." It gives you the mental time needed to just be you, and lets your eyes rest. No pretending, comparing, or trying to keep up with the Joneses. Just simple time to walk in the worthiness cycle with ease!

Phone a Friend

When you find yourself in the unworthiness cycle, phone a friend and tell them you need someone to listen. Ask them to set a timer for five minutes. You then have that time to share everything that is going wrong in your life—everything that is keeping you stuck in the unworthiness cycle. At the end of the five minutes, reset the timer and share everything that is going *right* in your life. This will get you back in the worthiness cycle.

Random Acts of Kindness

Be kind to yourself and others. Kindness emits a hormone called oxytocin. It is often called the love or kindness hormone and is a known antidote to depression. We are naturally wired to be kind—just like we are born worthy. We crave kindness. It is a natural part of the human condition. David Hamilton, author of *The 5 Side Effects of Kindness,* says, "When we are kind we feel happier and our bodies are healthiest. Kindness make us feel good. It alters the brain, dilates arteries, and lowers blood pressure."

When you are kind, you naturally stay in the worthiness cycle and you get healthier. Being unkind is unhealthy. Oxytocin actually softens the walls of the arteries in your heart so the heart does not have to work as hard to pump blood which in turn lowers your blood pressure. Kindness is like a muscle. If it goes unused, it atrophies. And kindness not only makes someone else's day better, it makes your day better, too. Practice random acts of kindness.

Ways to Be Kind

- Give someone a smile
- Hold the door for someone
- Rake your elderly neighbor's leaves
- Let someone in during rush hour
- Tell a bathroom cleaning lady how much you appreciate her
- Pay for the coffee of someone behind you in the coffee shop line
- Make a fresh pot of coffee at work
- Say "Thank You" more often

- Write a glowing review for a business online
- Offer words of encouragement
- Give a compliment
- Send flowers to a friend
- Bake cookies and give them away
- Congratulate someone

How do you practice kindness?

Say Yes, Yes, Yes

This one is for all you parents. When my son was small, I felt like all I ever did was tell him NO. But it didn't seem logical to spend so much time pointing out behaviors that were unacceptable or undesirable. Some days, it felt like *everything* he did was wrong and I wanted to teach him what the acceptable or desirable behavior could be instead. So, I started to catch him doing the behaviors I wanted, such as putting his toys away, being kind to friends, saying please and thank you, or setting the table for dinner. Soon enough, he did these more because he liked the positive affirmation. It's not easy to make the switch and there are times when a NO is going to be necessary. But remember that No, No, No can breed shame, guilt, and fear, while Yes, Yes, Yes is filled with possibility and positivity.

Hire a Coach

I am so grateful coaching does not just refer to sports anymore. Coaches specialize in helping you be the best you can be. A coach helps you take the journey from A to B. They hold you accountable to your commitments and call you on your bullshit. I would not be where I am today if it were not for the coaches that have been a part of my journey. There are many different types of coaches:

- Life Coaches
- Professional Coaches
- Relationship Coaches
- Transition Coaches
- Executive Coaches
- Health and Wellness Coaches
- Corporate Coaches
- Business Coaches
- Writing Coaches

When picking a coach, make sure you have a connection with them. What do you want your coach to help you with? Take some time and write a list of needs. Ask friends for referrals. Go to the websites of the coaches referred to you. Read their blogs, learn about their programs, and read the testimonials to get a feel for the person. Doing research upfront will save you a lot of time in the long run and help you get the coach that is right for you. I recommend interviewing a few before you choose the one that fits your needs.

Almost all coaches provide a complimentary or low-fee session for you to see if there is a connection. Many have a questionnaire for you to answer. Trust me, coaches do not want to work with someone who's not in their niche. They want to also have a connection with you and know that their services can benefit you in helping you on your journey. They want a win/win relationship for you and themselves.

For instance, I help people transform their relationship with worthiness so they can turn lives filled with hopelessness, exhaustion, and depression into lives filled with purpose, playfulness, and meaning. If someone came to me asking for help with bookkeeping, marketing, or how to start a business, it would not be a good fit for either of us.

I chose to work with a coach because I had tried to move from unworthiness to worthiness on my own. While I had some success, it was often short-lived. I had more false starts than needed because I was unable to be accountable to myself on a daily basis. I needed a coach to keep me accountable and give me tools I could add to my tool bag. I also wanted someone to cheer me on, celebrate my successes, and give me exercises to help me when I was stuck. And, yes, I wanted them to call me on my bullshit and give me a quick kick in the ass when I needed it. I also wanted someone who understood where I was and where I was going—someone who had taken a similar journey. I also wanted a coach who'd encourage me to be my own advocate, empower me to use my own tools, and help me be independent instead of codependent.

Having a coach can accelerate your forward progress. A coach will inspire, motivate, and empower you to step outside your uncomfortable comfort zone and into a comfortable comfort zone. They are your guide and can keep you from making the same missteps over and over.

When I met my stellar coach, Regena Garrepy, I was at an all-time low. Stuck in an unworthiness pattern that was not serving me, desperate for help and guidance. I was SO ready to commit to a guide that could help me get past myself. When I first spoke to her I just needed some guidance; I wasn't intending to ask her to be my coach. I don't think I even knew she was a coach at the time. She told me part of her story which made me feel connected to her because of our similarities. She offered me a complimentary session and gave me a document explaining her programs and a questionnaire that helped us determine if this would be a win/win relationship going forward.

I knew without a doubt that she was my coach and she knew that I was going to be a client she could assist on my journey. I would not be writing this book if it had not been for her coaching. Thank you, Regena!

SUMMARY

If you are in your golden years and think it is too late to make a change, think again. Louise Hay said her life did not start to have meaning until she was in her mid-forties. She began a writing career in her fifties. At fifty-five, she learned how to use computers even though she was afraid of them. She planted her first organic food garden at the age of sixty and started painting at this time, too. At seventy and eighty she felt more creative and that her life just kept getting richer and fuller every day. Now, no matter what your age, is the perfect time to realize you were born worthy!

CONCLUSION

Worthiness doesn't care who you are, where you came from, or how many failures you've had. It doesn't care whether you're rich or poor, tall or short, working or retired. Worthiness is available to all of us and you have the choice whether to see your own value or to stay stuck in the endless and painful cycle of unworthiness.

The journey to worthiness is the most important journey I've ever taken. In these challenging times, I believe it's what will help our world heal and thrive.

If you've read this far, hopefully you've decided to believe in yourself and ignite your worthiness.

And now you get to see what happens next as you use the tools in this book. The sky's the limit: Will your marriage go from dark and stormy to hot and steamy? Will your business grow to the next level creating financial abundance? Maybe you'll find yourself smiling more and enjoying each precious moment or planning that vacation you have talked about for decades.

I always see the last page of a book as the potential start of something new. My great wish is that this moment is the beginning of an abundant, meaningful, and unlimited life for you.

We all have blind spots. We get so stuck in our unworthy stories that we can't see what others see in us. And we miss the possibilities that are waiting for us. But the same story that keeps us in the unworthiness cycle also keeps us from making change.

So even though it may be scary to move away from your uncomfortable comfort zone, know that you now have the vision and the tools to break free from the unworthiness cycle—step into a new comfortable comfort zone and get different results.

I hope this book has inspired you to choose differently so you can create a different life, one in which you:

- Believe in yourself
- Love what you do
- Live life fully
- And most of all, KNOW THAT YOU ARE WORTHY OF THE LIFE YOU DREAM OF!

I am living proof that you can go from stumbling

through your days in a depleted state of unworthiness to thriving, fueled by the unlimited supply of worthiness that is your birthright. Let's put an end to the unworthiness epidemic right now.

Here's to your worthiness journey. May you create a life you can't wait to jump out of bed and live every day and help create a future in which worthiness is the way for each and every person.

You, my friend, are so, so WORTHY!

ABOUT THE AUTHOR

For 25 years, Julee Hunt worked way too many hours to prove she was worthy of success, love, and happiness. Then, as she approached the executive rungs on the corporate ladder, she was invited to leave her job. She walked away from the career that held her identity, happiness, and worthiness.

This sparked a journey of self-discovery, creating a life she desired, and giving up living according to others' standards. Today, Julee lives what she teaches and has made it her mission to end the Unworthiness Epidemic as she teaches others how to stay in the worthiness cycle. She speaks to audiences on how to believe in yourself, love what you do, and live life fully.

Julee and her husband are full-time RVers, traveling the country. For more information on her work, schedule, and availability to speak, visit

www. juleehuntinternational.com.

SPECIAL INVITATION
Complimentary A-HA Coaching Session

If you've decided to believe in yourself and ignite your worthiness, I invite you to apply for a complimentary A-HA session with me. In this private and confidential 1:1 session we take a look at what's keeping you in fear or holding you back from what you want.

What is one thing in your life that would change if you decided to ignite your worthiness and believe in yourself? This awareness could mark the beginning of a completely different life for you—one in which you know you *are* worthy of all you desire.

Because my time is limited, there's a short application process for the session, which you can complete here:

https://juleehuntinternational.com

click the "Apply Now" button

SPEAKING

Are you organizing a conference or retreat or looking for an entertaining, inspiring, and motivating speaker? In her warm, humorous presentations to women's groups, entrepreneurial meetings, church retreats and more, Julee shares the wisdom and healing power of her journey from unworthiness and a life of quiet desperation to worthiness and a life she can't wait to jump out of bed and live. She shines a light on how the world bombards us daily with self-defeating messages, and shares strategies for transforming those messages, identifying your triggers and becoming the leader of your life. Julee inspires audiences to remember that they *are* worthy and that when they recognize it, the whole world benefits.

The audience will learn:

- **The Unworthiness Cycle** – How great ideas start and eventually fizzle, squelching your dreams one by one.
- **The Worthiness Cycle** – How great ideas come to fruition allowing you to remember your worth and manifest your dreams.
- **The Daily Worthiness Workout** – How to reignite your worthiness and combat all the "you're not enough" messages.

- **What it Takes to Be a Worthiness Warrior** – How to have more impact and help our world thrive.

To request Julee as a speaker, fill out this short form:

<u>juleehuntinternational.com</u>

click "Book Julee"